A variety collection of six Christmas programs for the church family

L.G. ENSCOE
&
ANNIE ENSCOE

MERIWETHER PUBLISHING LTD.
Colorado Springs, Colorado

Meriwether Publishing Ltd., Publisher
Box 7710
Colorado Springs, CO 80933

Editor: Rhonda Wray
Typesetting: Sharon E. Garlock
Cover design: Tom Myers
Cover photo: Drew Meredith (cover photographer) in scene from *The Towne Without a Tale*
Interior book photographs: Annie Enscoe, Drew Meredith, Dan McGowan, and Jeff Firestone Photography

Library of Congress Cataloging-in-Publication Data

Enscoe, Lawrence G.
    Joy to the world! : a variety collection of Christmas programs for the church family / L. G. Enscoe and Annie Enscoe.
      p.   cm.
    ISBN 1-56608-005-3 : $12.95
    1. Christmas plays, American. 2. Christian drama, American.
I. Enscoe, Andrea J.   II. Title.
PS3555.N74J69   1994
812'.54--dc20   94-23107
                                              CIP

This book is dedicated

To all the voices at GPC
who have made Christmas joyous for so many.

But especially for us.

Thank you for your
talent, hard work, and patience.

C'mon, people, move with purpose . . .

CONTENTS

FOREWORD

The programs you will find in this book have been a Christmas-time rallying point at Glendale Presbyterian Church since 1989. The congregation looks forward to what they will see every year. With these scripts, new energy has been created for evangelism. I am most pleased that they attract the community, neighbors, and friends in the workplace.

They have also been a privilege to participate in. These events have always drawn in my family, and they involved so many people in our church family — from production planning, set building and selling tickets, to staging the final performance.

People come to see these programs because of the creative approach to the Gospel story that Larry and Annie provide. The Enscoes keep the story fresh and relevant.

With this kind of material as a start, the church might again take the lead in the arts.

Ralph Winter
Producer, Walt Disney Studios

Some of Mr. Winter's films include: *Star Trek IV: The Voyage Home, Star Trek VI: The Undiscovered Country, Explorers, Flight of the Intruder, Captain Ron,* and the upcoming Disney film, Robert A. Heinlein's *The Puppetmasters.*

PREFACE

For thirty years Glendale Presbyterian Church in Glendale, California has been inviting the community into its cathedral-style stone sanctuary to celebrate Christmas through family programs of drama and song.

And they keep coming back.

They know they'll hear music they've never heard before, and songs they've loved for years. They know they'll see artful costumes, colorful sets and engaging stories. And they know they'll experience an exuberance and sincerity about the One we especially adore this time of year.

Between these covers are some of those programs.

Call for the Lights and Sing is a bustling medieval fest where three Knaves interrupt the King's party to tell the real story of Christmas. *The Wise Men Had It Easy* is a seriously comic look at our favorite Christmas pastime: shopping. *The King Who Hated Christmas* is a fractured fairy tale about a King who finds out who *really* reigns. *The Great Gemdale Christmas Tree Ornament Factory* is a hip contemporary story about the diversity in God's people at Christmas. *The Towne Without a Tale* is a comic tale about a medieval town putting on its own Christmas pageant. And finally, *Candles and Carols* is a traditional family Christmas celebration.

In putting these programs together, we wanted to tell a familiar story in a way that would delight, move and surprise.

We understood people would come into our midst who knew nothing about the birth of Christ, and then there would be those who have heard the story all their lives.

We understood families would come, with a diversity of ages and ethnic groups — people with a wide range of musical and theatrical experience.

We understood people would be tired. Harried. Inundated with the stuff of Christmas — both secular and sacred.

And we understood people wanted to walk out into the brisk

1

Christmas air invigorated, changed, uplifted and hopeful.

We wish you laughter, tears, hard work, and life-changing moments with the God who "lit up the world from dusk to dawn" in a small hill town called Bethlehem.

Larry & Annie Enscoe
July, 1994

CALL FOR THE LIGHTS AND SING!

A Medieval Christmas
Festival
of
Carols and Drama

L. G. Enscoe
Annie Enscoe

Photo: Dan McGowan

Jeff Witzeman (L) and Eric Loomis in a scene from the Glendale
Presbyterian Church production of *Call for the Lights and Sing!*

CALL FOR THE LIGHTS AND SING!

CAST

KNAVE ONE

KNAVE TWO

KNAVE THREE

KING

QUEEN

SINGERS

CHOIR DIRECTOR

PAGES/JUGGLERS

THE PARSON

A brass ensemble adds a nice flourish to the drama,
if musicians are available.

PRODUCTION NOTES

Running Time

Seventy to eighty minutes.

Props

Two handbells; two royal thrones; greenery; hourglass; wooden wassail bowls; wooden pitchers; banners (The banners may be made of colorful material cut in a triangle or rectangle and mounted on poles. They may be plain or have medieval heraldic symbols sewn on if desired.); two wooden crates; a scroll; a battered wooden mallet; a trunk; "Twelve Days of Christmas" joke props (Five onion rings, two berets, four cellular phones, six L'eggs pantyhose containers, eleven pipes, nine lacy bonnets, etc.); three paper crowns; a doll wrapped in a blanket to represent the baby Jesus; small percussive instruments.

Costumes

The Singers (Choir) as well as the King, Queen, Knaves, Choir Director, Pages, Jugglers and the Parson are all dressed in medieval clothes. Specialty patterns may be found in fabric stores for most of these. Use peasant dresses for the women and breeches cut off at the knees, high stockings, and a poncho-type shirt tied with rope or a leather belt for the men. You can find books of costumes in theatre or college bookstores to get ideas for medieval costumes. Pay particular attention to the fifteenth and sixteenth centuries. Otherwise, you can rent your costumes, which is the route we always took. The salesperson can help you locate the costume that fits your character.

The Knaves are dressed in low-rent peasant clothes. When the Knaves play biblical characters, they wear the appropriate piece of costume. The Shepherds wear old robes or headpieces and ties, the Wise Men wear royal cloaks and paper crowns. Joseph puts on a rough robe. When Knave Three plays the Announcer, he wears a page hat and short cloak.

The King and Queen look very regal. The Choir Director can be dressed like a courtier, or a mistress in an up-scale medieval gown with a flower wreath in her hair. Pages are dressed like

6

pages; Jugglers like jesters. The Parson can wear a clerical robe or be dressed like a monk.

Set

We performed the program with a bare platform and two large royal-looking chairs. We used risers for the Singers. We covered the risers in a tarp material painted to look like they were made of stone. All locations (i.e. Bethlehem and the stable) are pantomimed — no sets are required for them.

SUGGESTED MUSIC SOURCES

The following is a listing of the music used in the original production of *Call for the Lights and Sing!*

"I Hear the Minstrels in Our Streets," arr. Donald Waxman, Galaxy Music.

"Masters in This Hall," arr. David Willcocks, Oxford University Press.

"Wassail Song," arr. Donald Waxman, Galaxy Music (also found in *The Oxford Book of Carols*).

"Deck the Halls," arr. Alice Parker and Robert Shaw, published by Lawson Gould/G. Schirmer.

"Twelve Days of Christmas," arr. Alice Parker and Robert Shaw; G. Schirmer.

"Lord of the Dance" is a traditional Shaker tune and can be found in hymnals or the Young Life song book.

"The Holly and the Ivy," *Oxford Book of Carols*.

"O Little Town of Bethlehem," arr. Kay Hawkes Goodyear, Chapel Hill Music (or any hymnal).

"Infant Holy, Infant Lowly," arr. David Willcocks, "Carols for Choirs 1," Oxford University Press (and many hymnals).

"Coventry Carol," arr. Donald Waxman, Galaxy Music (or in the *Oxford Book of Carols*).

"To Us Is Born Immanuel," arr. Michael Praetorius and Walter Buszin, published by Schmitt, Hall & McCreary.

"Hark! the Herald Angels Sing," *Oxford Book of Carols* (and most hymnals).

"While by My Sheep," 17th century, arr. Hugo Jungst.

"The Coming of Our King," Polish Traditional, arr. John Rutter, Hinshaw Music.

"We Three Kings" (can be found in most hymnals and *The Oxford Book of Carols*).

"Joy to the World," arr. Gordon Young, Fred Bock Music Co. (and most hymnals).

"We Wish You a Merry Christmas," arr. John Rutter, Hinshaw Music Co.

AUTHORS' NOTES

"Call for the Lights and Sing!" is a medieval family Christmas festival that mixes colorful fun, powerful evangelism and a lot of familiar carols and hymns. It can be staged in the sanctuary or in a fellowship hall. Lighting instructions are included to enhance the drama, but they are not vital if you don't have theatrical lighting.

The songs listed were used in the original production, and give an idea of the kind of message and tone required at that point in the story. Please feel free to choose your own music, or to add music if you want to make it a longer program. Remember to print the lyrics for any songs the congregation will be singing in your program.

The "Welcome All!" poem used near the beginning of the program is from Kenneth Grahame's "The Wind in the Willows." The Scripture story the Knaves repeat is from Luke 2:8-18. The closing benediction is from a salutation Fra Giovanni wrote to a friend in 1513.

A final word: this play is designed to be boisterous, colorful, and festive. Encourage clapping, singing along, mingling in the audience, and, where it's appropriate, lots of comic bits for the Knaves and Jugglers.

Thou havest a good time, ya hear?

9

CALL FOR THE LIGHTS AND SING!

A Medieval Christmas
Festival
of
Carols and Drama

SCENE ONE
"The Knaves A-Plotting"

SCENE TWO
"The Blessing and Festivities of the Hall"

SCENE THREE
"Enter Christmas"

SCENE FOUR
"Carols and Benedictions"

1 **SCENE ONE**
2 **"The Knaves A-Plotting"**
3
4 *(The playing area or sanctuary platform is clear, except for choir*
5 *risers or levels which may be covered with material and painted*
6 *to look like stone, and two large throne-like chairs. Greens and*
7 *decorations bedeck the place.*
8 *(After a moment, a single instrument begins playing, "O Come,*
9 *O Come, Emmanuel" from some unseen place. It's haunting and*
10 *compelling.*
11 *(At the close of the music, a hand with a bell suddenly pops out*
12 *from behind one of the massive chairs. The bell is rung.*
13 *(Nothing happens. A face appears over the top of the chair and*
14 *looks around, dismayed. He rings the bell again. Nothing. What*
15 *is going on? He stomps out onto the stage.*
16 *(This is KNAVE ONE, a servant in the royal hall dressed in*
17 *medieval peasant clothes. He's upset. He rings the bell again.*
18 *Louder. Now he's really upset.*
19 *(Just as he is about to ring again, two hands with hand bells*
20 *pop out on either side of the other massive chair. Faces pop over*
21 *the top of the chair.)*
22 **KNAVE ONE: My friends!** *(KNAVE TWO and KNAVE THREE*
23 *run out to meet KNAVE ONE. It's a flurry of activity. They hug,*
24 *exchange presents, greet each other with "Merry Christmas!" and*
25 *Olde English salutations. Apparently, they think there is no*
26 *audience watching.)* **Friends, friends!** *(They look at him.)* **Are**
27 **we rehearsed for our parts?**
28 **KNAVE TWO: I have been well-studied in the roles I will**
29 **dissemble.**
30 **KNAVE THREE: Indeed! I've got my lines down cold-eth!**
31 **KNAVE ONE: All is well then!**
32 **KNAVE THREE:** *(Glum)* **Ahhh, wherefore all our pains, my**
33 **friends? Our king would never allow his lowly servants**
34 **to take part in these yuletide festivities.**
35 **KNAVE TWO: By my troth, year upon year, the Old Man**

13

1   **throws an office Christmas party, and we're not even on**
2   **the guest list-eth.**
3   **KNAVE ONE:**   **Nay, this year will see a new course, my**
4   **cronies! This Christmas Eve our message of the manger**
5   **will be told! Our scenes of light will not go unplayed.**
6   **Even a king is not above hearing such a tale.**
7   **KNAVE THREE:**   **Alas . . . we can only hope there will be an**
8   **audience to share in our —** *(KNAVE THREE sees the*
9   *congregation. He freezes. The other KNAVES look at him oddly.*
10   *They look at what he's looking at. They see the congregation.)*
11   **KNAVES ONE and TWO:**   **Whoooa-eth!**
12   **KNAVE TWO:**   **Where didst they come from?**
13   **KNAVE THREE:**   **The place-eth is packed!**
14   **KNAVE TWO:**   **By my troth, these must be early.**
15   **KNAVE ONE:**   *(Pulls out an hourglass and reads it.)* **Not so, my**
16   **chums! They are here at the appointed time. It is the king**
17   **and his court who tarry!**
18   **KNAVE TWO:**   **Still wassailing all over the town, if it must be**
19   **known.**
20   **KNAVE THREE:**   *(Acting!)* **Ah . . . an audience! An** *audience!*
21   **At last our little company will have willing ears waiting**
22   **to see the hard work we have —** *(A brass fanfare from the*
23   *back of the hall cuts him off.)* **I knewest 'twas too good to be**
24   **true.**
25   **KNAVE ONE:**   *(Excited)* **'Tis no matter! Now we must return to**
26   **our work! Anon! For on this Christmas Eve, we shall**
27   **remember the one who made stars stand still and stiff**
28   **knees bend in adoration!**
29   **KNAVE TWO:**   *(Impressed)* **Ewww. Not bad, Ernie.**
30   **KNAVE ONE:**   **I thank thee! And now — away!** *(The KNAVES*
31   *scatter in different directions.)*
32
33
34
35

1	**SCENE TWO**
2	"The Blessings and Festivities of the Hall"
3	
4	*(Bright lights come up.*
5	*(The BRASS ENSEMBLE enters the hall, playing a lively*
6	*fanfare.*
7	*(The SINGERS [Choir] enter, moving up the aisles, greeting the*
8	*congregation and singing, "I Hear the Minstrels in Our Street"*
9	*[or another suitably bright entrance tune].*
10	*(The CHOIR DIRECTOR walks in front, directing the*
11	*SINGERS.*
12	*(JUGGLERS bring up the rear. It's all very colorful and*
13	*festive.*
14	*(Finally, the platform is filled with SINGERS, clapping and*
15	*smiling. The JUGGLERS move among them.)*
16	*SONG:* "I Hear the Minstrels in Our Street."
17	**SINGERS:** *(Singing)* **I hear the minstrels in our street.**
18	**O listen to the oboes playing sweet Noels.**
19	**And we listen, O listen, listen, O listen,**
20	**Hear them passing by,**
21	**Hear the minstrels in our street.**
22	
23	**Hear them, O hear them, hear them, O hear them,**
24	**Hear, O hear them playing sweet Noels.**
25	
26	**Each year the Noels ring out**
27	**From ev'ry village street.**
28	**The singers raise their voices**
29	**Full and rich in sound;**
30	**And we too will sing by the fire,**
31	**Sing until the midnight hour.**
32	
33	**Ring out, O ring out,**
34	**Ring out, O ring out,**
35	**Ring out, all the sweet Noels.**

15

1   The Shepherds in their fields
2   Regard the infant boy.
3   The shepherds in their fields
4   Regard the infant boy;
5   They sing to him their praises,
6   Sing to him their joy.
7

8   And we too will sing by the fire,
9   Sing, will sing until the midnight hour.
10   Listen, O listen, listen, O listen,
11   Listen to the sweet Noels.
12

13   There is a poor old woman
14   Who washes by the stream;
15   She hears the minstrels playing
16   When she is by the stream.
17

18   And though the wind is icy,
19   Warm she feels within;
20   Just as warm'd by the fire
21   When we sing till the midnight hour.
22   Until the midnight hour!
23   *(When the song is over, the SINGERS turn to the audience and*
24   *say:)*
25 **SINGERS:**   *(Speaking)* **Welcome all!**
26 **WOMEN:**   *(Speaking)* **Welcome all, this frosty tide.**
27   Let your doors swing open wide
28   That wind may follow and snow beside
29   And draw us in by your fire to bide.
30   Joy shall be yours in the morning!
31 **MEN:**   *(Speaking)* **Here we stand in the cold and the sleet,**
32   Glowing fingers and stamping feet.
33   Come from far away you to greet
34   You by the fire and we in the street
35   Bidding you joy in the morning!

1   **CHOIR DIRECTOR:**   *(To the audience)* **Please, to your feet one**
2   **and all, that we might bid welcome to the Masters of the**
3   **Hall!**
4   *(The BRASS ENSEMBLE strikes an introduction as the*
5   *audience is encouraged to stand.*
6   *(The SINGERS sing "Master in This Hall" [or some other stately*
7   *medieval carol]. Some play tambourines, small drums and other*
8   *percussive instruments.*
9   *(The KING and QUEEN process up the center aisle. They are*
10   *dressed in gorgeous regalia, majestically nodding to the*
11   *congregation as they pass. Two PAGES with banners follow behind.*
12   *(The KNAVES bring up the rear, carrying large wooden pitchers.*
13   *They encourage the congregation to sing the refrain.)*
14   *SONG:*   "Masters in This Hall"
15   **SINGERS:**   *(Singing)* **Masters in this hall,**
16   **Hear ye news today**
17   **Brought from oversea:**
18
19   **Nowell! Nowell! Nowell!**
20   **Nowell sing we clear!**
21   **Holpen are all folk on earth,**
22   **Born is God's Son so dear:**
23
24   **Nowell! Nowell! Nowell!**
25   **Nowell sing we loud!**
26   **God today hath poor folk raised**
27   **And cast a-down the proud.**
28
29   **Going o'er the hills,**
30   **Through the milk-white snow,**
31   **Hear the ewes bleat**
32   **While the wind did blow.**
33
34   **REFRAIN:**   **Shepherds many an' one**
35   **Sat among the sheep,**

.

1	No man spake more word
2	Than they had been asleep.
3	
4	REFRAIN: Quoth I, "Fellows Mine,
5	Why this guise sit ye?
6	Making but dull cheer,
7	Shepherds though ye be?"
8	
9	REFRAIN: "Shepherds should of right
10	Leap and dance and sing,
11	Thus to see ye sit,
12	Is a right strange thing."
13	
14	REFRAIN: Quoth these fellows then,
15	"To Bethlehem town we go,
16	To see a mighty Lord
17	Lie in a manger low."
18	
19	REFRAIN: "How name ye this lord,
20	Shepherds?" then said I,
21	"Very God," they said,
22	"Come from heaven high."
23	
24	REFRAIN: This is Christ the Lord,
25	Masters be ye glad!
26	Christmas is come in,
27	And no folk should be sad.
28	*(At the close of the song, the entourage is positioned on the stage.*
29	*The KING and QUEEN are Down Front, flanked by PAGES.*
30	*The KNAVES stand off to the side.)*
31	KING: I bid thee full welcome to this great hall.
32	Where words and music are meant to enthrall.
33	Christmastide here seek we to uphold
34	While winter crawls close with numbing cold.
35	So fill your glasses, your hearts with good cheer.

1   **Celebrate the God who to us draws near.**
2   **We'll sing. We'll dance. We'll laugh with hearts full**
3   **And so worship our Lord on this joyous glad Yule!**
4   *(The QUEEN comes up next to him.)*
5   QUEEN: **Indeed, husband, look we first to the one in prayer,**
6   **Whose blessing we seek, standing full in his care.**
7   KING: **By my troth, good lady, thou hast giv'n the call.**
8   **Be there a parson in the hall?** *(Everyone looks to the*
9   *MINISTER, seated in the front row. If desired, the MINISTER*
10   *can be dressed like a medieval monk or parson. The MINISTER*
11   *offers the welcome and opening prayer. At the close, the KING*
12   *shakes the MINISTER's hand. The MINISTER then takes a seat.)*
13   KING: **I thank thee, Parson** *(Your minister's name)* _____.
14   *(He turns to the congregation.)* **And now, let's wassail again**
15   **as we did last Christmas!**
16   *(The SINGERS begin "The Wassail Song." During the song, the*
17   *KING and QUEEN process to their thrones and sit. The*
18   *SINGERS hold up wooden bowls and the KNAVES rush in to*
19   *pantomime filling each one with wassail. When they are done,*
20   *the KNAVES bustle out of the hall.)*
21   *SONG:*   "The Wassail Song."
22   SINGERS: *(Singing)* **Here we come-a-wassailing**
23   **Among the leaves so green,**
24   **Here we come a-wand'ring**
25   **So fair to be seen.**
26
27   **Love and joy come to you,**
28   **And to you your wassail too;**
29   **And God bless you, and send you a happy new year.**
30   **And God send you a happy new year.**
31
32   **O here we go a-wassailing**
33   **Among the leaves so green,**
34   **O here we come a-wand'ring**
35   **So fair to be seen.**

1	Love and joy come to you,
2	And to you your wassail too;
3	And God bless you and send you a happy new year,
4	And God send you a happy new year!
5	
6	Our wassail cup is made of the rosemary tree,
7	Our wassail cheer is made from the best barley.
8	
9	Love and joy come to you,
10	And to you your wassail too;
11	And God bless you and send you a happy new year,
12	And God send you a happy new year!
13	
14	God bless the master of this house,
15	And bless the mistress too,
16	And all the little children
17	That round the table go.
18	
19	Love and joy come to you,
20	And to you your wassail too,
21	And God bless you and send you a happy new year,
22	And God send you a happy new year!
23	*(At the close of the song, the QUEEN stands and faces the*
24	*congregation.)*
25	QUEEN: 'Tis, indeed, a time of joy and festivity!
26	As we remember the day of our Lord's Nativity!
27	Hide no mirth when the singers call!
28	Like the holly, our voices shall deck the hall!
29	*(The SINGERS begin "Deck the Halls." They bid the*
30	*congregation to join them in the carol. As they sing, some of the*
31	*SINGERS can decorate the stage with more evergreen. The*
32	*JUGGLERS weave among the people. It's a very festive moment.)*
33	*SONG:* "Deck the Halls."
34	SINGERS and CONGREGATION: *(Singing)* Deck the halls
35	with boughs of holly,

1	Fa la la la la, la la la la.
2	'Tis the season to be jolly,
3	Fa la la la la, la la la la.
4	Don we now our gay apparel,
5	Fa la la la la, la la la la.
6	Troll the ancient Yuletide carol,
7	Fa la la la la, la la la la.
8	
9	See the blazing Yule before us,
10	Fa la la la la, la la la la.
11	Strike the harp and join the chorus,
12	Fa la la la la, la la la la.
13	Follow me in merry measure,
14	Fa la la la la, la la la la.
15	While I tell of Christmas treasure,
16	Fa la la la la, la la la la.
17	
18	Fast away the old year passes,
19	Fa la la la la, la la la la.
20	Hail the new, ye lads and lasses,
21	Fa la la la la, la la la la.
22	Sing we joyous all together,
23	Fa la la la la, la la la la.
24	Heedless of the wind or weather,
25	Fa la la la la, la la la la.
26	*(At the close of the carol, KNAVE TWO and KNAVE THREE*
27	*walk onto the platform, dragging a trunk. Everyone looks*
28	*surprised.)*
29	**KING: Ho, there, Knaves.**
30	**KNAVES:** *(Quickly bowing)* **Yes, sire?**
31	**KING: What art thou doing?**
32	**KNAVE TWO:** *(Bowing)* **We have a number we'd liketh to do**
33	**for you.** *(The KING looks at the QUEEN. She smiles and nods*
34	*at the KNAVES.)*
35	**QUEEN: Proceed, friends.** *(The KNAVES look at each other.*

1   *They can't believe their good fortune.)*
2   **KING:**   **Well, what art thou waiting for?**
3   **KNAVE TWO:**   *(Grinning; to CHOIR DIRECTOR)* **Hit-eth it!**
4   *(The music begins for "Twelve Days of Christmas." The*
5   *SINGERS take up the song. The KNAVES open the trunk and*
6   *begin their routine. As each gift is mentioned in the song, the*
7   *KNAVES act it out: One KNAVE jumping into the other's arms*
8   *for "partridge in a pear tree." Onion rings for "five golden rings."*
9   *Berets for "French hens." Cellular phones for "calling birds."*
10   *L'eggs pantyhose egg-shaped containers for "geese a-laying."*
11   *Tobacco pipes for "pipers." Lacy bonnets for "ladies dancing."*
12   *The jokes are found in making contemporary and/or literal props*
13   *for each element of the song. It gets wilder as the song gets faster*
14   *and more complicated. Soon they are tossing props down and*
15   *snapping them up at lightning speed to keep up with the lyrics.)*
16   *SONG:*   "The Twelve Days of Christmas."
17   **SINGERS:**   *(Singing)* **On the first day of Christmas**
18   **My true love sent to me**
19   **A partridge in a pear tree.**
20
21   **On the second day of Christmas**
22   **My true love sent to me**
23   **Two turtledoves,**
24   **And a partridge in a pear tree.**
25
26   **On the third day of Christmas**
27   **My true love sent to me**
28   **Three French hens,**
29   **Two turtledoves,**
30   **And a partridge in a pear tree.**
31
32   **On the fourth day of Christmas**
33   **My true love sent to me**
34   **Four calling birds,**
35   **Three French hens,**

1	Two turtledoves,
2	And a partridge in a pear tree.
3	
4	On the fifth day of Christmas
5	My true love sent to me
6	Five golden rings!
7	Four calling birds,
8	Three French hens,
9	Two turtledoves,
10	And a partridge in a pear tree.
11	
12	On the sixth day of Christmas
13	My true love sent to me
14	Six geese a-laying,
15	Five golden rings!
16	Four calling birds,
17	Three French hens,
18	Two turtledoves,
19	And a partridge in a pear tree.
20	
21	On the seventh day of Christmas
22	My true love sent to me
23	Seven swans a-swimming,
24	Six geese a-laying,
25	Five golden rings!
26	Four calling birds,
27	Three French hens,
28	Two turtledoves,
29	And a partridge in a pear tree.
30	
31	On the eighth day of Christmas
32	My true love sent to me
33	Eight maids a-milking,
34	Seven swans a-swimming,
35	Six geese a-laying,

1	Five golden rings!
2	Four calling birds,
3	Three French hens,
4	Two turtledoves,
5	And a partridge in a pear tree.
6	
7	On the ninth day of Christmas
8	My true love sent to me
9	Nine ladies dancing,
10	Eight maids a-milking,
11	Seven swans a-swimming,
12	Six geese a-laying,
13	Five golden rings!
14	Four calling birds,
15	Three French hens,
16	Two turtledoves,
17	And a partridge in a pear tree.
18	
19	On the tenth day of Christmas
20	My true love sent to me
21	Ten lords a-leaping,
22	Nine ladies dancing,
23	Eight maids a-milking,
24	Seven swans a-swimming,
25	Six geese a-laying,
26	Five golden rings!
27	Four calling birds,
28	Three French hens,
29	Two turtledoves,
30	And a partridge in a pear tree.
31	
32	On the eleventh day of Christmas
33	My true love sent to me
34	Eleven pipers piping,
35	Ten lords a-leaping,

1   Nine ladies dancing,
2   Eight maids a-milking,
3   Seven swans a-swimming,
4   Six geese a-laying,
5   Five golden rings!
6   Four calling birds,
7   Three French hens,
8   Two turtledoves,
9   And a partridge in a pear tree.
10
11   On the twelfth day of Christmas
12   My true love sent to me
13   Twelve drummers drumming,
14   Eleven pipers piping,
15 • Ten lords a-leaping,
16   Nine ladies dancing,
17   Eight maids a-milking,
18   Seven swans a-swimming,
19   Six geese a-laying,
20   Five golden rings!
21   Four calling birds,
22   Three French hens,
23   Two turtledoves,
24   And a partridge in a pear tree.
25   *(At the final "partridge in a pear tree," the two KNAVES collapse*
26   *in exhaustion. The SINGERS laugh and applaud. The KNAVES*
27   *stand and bow to the SINGERS and the KING and QUEEN.*
28   *(A SOLOIST immediately begins to sing. Suggested song —*
29   *"Lord of the Dance." The SINGERS join the SOLOIST, moving*
30   *out into the aisles, caught up in the song. Some use the percussion*
31   *instruments again. Others clap. At the close, there is applause*
32   *and cheering.*
33   *(Another medieval-like carol can be included here — perhaps a*
34   *SOLOIST singing "The Holly and the Ivy" while the SINGERS*
35   *remain standing in the aisles, singing the refrain. When the*

1   *singing is done, the SINGERS head back to the platform, still*
2   *laughing and talking.)*
3
4
5
6
7
8
9
10
11
12
13
14
15
16
17
18
19
20
21
22
23
24
25
26
27
28
29
30
31
32
33
34
35

SCENE THREE
"Enter Christmas"

(Based on the Luke and Matthew accounts of Jesus' birth, King James Version.)

(As the SINGERS return to the platform, KNAVE THREE elbows his way through the crowd, wearing a page's cloak and hat, and carrying a wooden crate.)

KNAVE THREE: *(Cockney accent)* **Pardon me! Excuse me! Out of the way! Pardon me!** *(KNAVE THREE makes his way to the platform and slaps the crate down. No one notices him. They're still talking and laughing. KNAVE THREE steps up on the crate and looks around. He clears his throat. No reaction. Finally, KNAVE THREE in booming voice:)* **'Ear ye! 'Ear ye!** *(Everyone turns and looks at him. KNAVE THREE smiles, smugly.)* **Now the Birf' of Jesus came about likewise and in this manner!** *(He unfurls a scroll that rolls down past his feet and off the stage. The SINGERS and the KING and QUEEN laugh.)* **The book of the generations of Jesus Christ, the son of David, the son of Abraham!** *(Reading down the list)* **Now, Abraham begat-eth Isaac, Isaac begat-eth Jacob, Jacob begat-eth Judah and 'is brovers, Judah begat ...** *(The SINGERS groan. Some begin to fall asleep. KNAVE THREE goes on bravely.)* **And Judah begat-eth Phares and Zara of Thamar, and Phares begat-eth Esrom, and Esrom begat-eth Aram, and Aram begat-eth ... he begat-eth ...** *(KNAVE THREE looks around. Everyone is snoring.)* **But ... but I 'ave more begat-eths!**

QUEEN: **Skip a few verses, good sir.** *(KNAVE THREE looks hurt, but adjusts. He looks down the scroll.)*

KNAVE THREE: **Lemme see 'ere ... begat-eth ... uh, begat-eth ... begat-eth ... ah, here we are ...** *(He clears his throat.)* **'Ear ye! 'Ear ye!** *(The SINGERS all snap awake. KNAVE THREE gives them another smug smile and begins to proclaim.)* **And it came to pass-eth in those days that there**

27

1   **went out a decree from Caesar Augustus that all the**

2   **world should be taxed!** *(Aside)* **Now mind you, this taxin'**

3   **first took place while Cyrenius was the bloomin' gov'nuh**

4   **o' Syria.** *(Back to the scroll)* **And Joseph also went up from**

5   **Galilee, out of the city of Nazaref ', into Judea, to the city**

6   **of David, which is called Beflehem ... because 'e was of**

7   **the 'ouse and lineage of David ... to be taxed wif ' Mary**

8   **his espoused wife, bein' great wif ' child.** *(The music begins*

9   *for "O Little Town of Bethlehem." KNAVE THREE plops down*

10   *on the box and rolls up the scroll. KNAVE ONE comes in, wearing*

11   *a tattered cloak, a battered wooden mallet stuck in his belt. He*

12   *is playing Joseph. While he speaks, he pantomimes helping Mary*

13   *lie down in the imaginary straw of the stable.)*

14 **KNAVE ONE:**   **And so it was, that while they were there, the**

15   **days were accomplished that she should be delivered.**

16   **And she brought forth her first-born son, and wrapped**

17   **him in swaddling clothes, and laid him in a manger ...**

18   *(KNAVE ONE looks at KNAVE TWO, who rudely turns his*

19   *back to him. KNAVE ONE sits sadly.)* **Because there was no**

20   **room for them in the inn.** (Luke 2:6, 7) *(The lights go out on*

21   *the KNAVES and come up on the SINGERS.)*

22 *SONG:*   "O Little Town of Bethlehem."

23 **SINGERS:**   *(Singing)* **O little town of Bethlehem**

24   **How still we see thee lie.**

25   **Above the deep and dreamless sleep**

26   **The silent stars go by.**

27

28   **Yet in thy dark streets shineth**

29   **The everlasting Light.**

30   **The hopes and fears of all the years**

31   **Are met in thee tonight.**

32

33   **For Christ is born of Mary,**

34   **And gathered all above,**

35   **While mortals sleep, the angels keep**

1   Their watch of wondering love.
2
3   O morning stars, together
4   Proclaim the holy birth!
5   And praises sing to God the King,
6   And peace to men on earth.
7
8   How silently, how silently,
9   The wondrous gift is giv'n
10 So God imparts to human hearts
11 The blessings of his heaven.
12
13 No ear may hear his coming,
14 But in this world of sin,
15 Where meek souls will receive him still,
16 The dear Christ enters in.
17
18 O holy Child of Bethlehem!
19 Descend on us, we pray;
20 Cast out our sin and enter in,
21 Be born in us today.
22
23 We hear the Christmas angels
24 The great glad tidings tell;
25 O come to us, abide with us,
26 Our Lord Emmanuel!
27 *(This carol is followed by a duet of "Infant Holy, Infant Lowly.")*
28 *SONG:* "Infant Holy, Infant Lowly."
29 Infant holy, infant lowly
30 For his bed a cradle stall;
31 Oxen lowing, little knowing
32 Christ, the babe, is Lord of all.
33
34 Swift are winging, angels singing
35 Noels ringing, tidings bringing

1	Christ the babe is Lord of all.
2	
3	Flocks were sleeping, shepherds keeping
4	Vigil till the morning new
5	Saw the glory, heard the story,
6	Tidings of a gospel true.
7	
8	Thus rejoicing, free from sorrow,
9	Praises voicing, greet the morrow:
10	Christ the babe was born for you,
11	Christ the babe was born for you.
12	*(At the close of the duet, KNAVE ONE comes forward holding*
13	*the bundled child.)*
14	KNAVE ONE: Joseph, thou son of David, fear not to take
15	unto thee Mary thy wife: for that which is conceived in
16	her is of the Holy Ghost. And she shall bring forth a son,
17	and thou shalt call his name Jesus: for he shall save his
18	people from their sins. (Matthew 1:20, 21) *(KNAVE ONE*
19	*cradles the child as the WOMEN sing an a cappella version of*
20	*the "Coventry Carol." During the carol, the lights fade out on*
21	*KNAVE ONE.)*
22	*SONG:* "Coventry Carol."
23	WOMEN: *(Singing)* Lully, lulla thou little tiny child,
24	By, by lully lullay
25	O sisters too, how may we do
26	For to preserve this day.
27	This poor youngling we do sing,
28	By, by lully lullay?
29	
30	Lully, lulla
31	By, by lully lullay.
32	O sisters too, how may we do
33	For to preserve this day.
34	This poor youngling
35	For whom we do sing?

1   By, by
2   By, by lully lullay?
3   *(The lights fade on the platform. A pause. In the darkness we*
4   *hear the sound of nailing. Lights pick up KNAVE ONE, still as*
5   *Joseph. He's sitting on the ground, hammering a nail into the*
6   *crate. He looks up at the congregation.)*
7 **KNAVE ONE:**   I like it not! He shall not stay in a manger, like
8   some newborn animal that surprised its master with a
9   hasty appearance. *(He holds up the crate, which signifies the*
10   *beginning work on a cradle.)* **By morn, I shall have builded**
11   him this cradle. 'Tis the very least I can give him since I
12   have naught else. *(He sighs and shakes his head.)*
13   Money. 'Tis the alchemy I would need to have
14   changed this base element. I might have sweetly paid for
15   a bed, a candle, a bowl of warming soup. But nothing of
16   the like is here. Filth, rough straw, our breaths hung
17   coldly in the air. This seems to be our reward for true
18   fidelity. *(He hammers a moment, then looks off.)*
19   That rich innkeeper's wife surely hath a soft pillow
20   whereupon to lie her head. What have I for my Mary?
21   Stones. That is what *I* offer. Stones wrapped in birth-
22   soaked garments. Stones like Jacob found fleeing in the
23   desert. Only here there is but silence with the icy rock.
24   No ladders of heaven. No angels descending to greet this
25   promise. Angels once greeted us. Once calmed us with
26   words of peace when our bodies rattled with fear.
27   "Mary . . . thou art highly favored." Well, now I am sore
28   afraid. *(He looks up.)* **Where are the angels?!** *(He works on*
29   *the crate for a moment.)*
30   By my troth, I cannot conceive of a promise that
31   could be fulfilled with such a beginning as this. *(To God)*
32   What is thy mind? Would any mortal give ear to a man
33   who smells of a birth in such a place? Will they heed him
34   in age when they have hailed him with bolted doors as
35   a babe? *(He sets a nail against the cradle leg.)*

1   I say this: If thy created world could not find room
2   for a child in the blackness of midnight — what shall they
3   do when they receive the daylit news that he is the Son of
4   God? *(At that, KNAVE ONE begins hammering the nail in. We*
5   *listen to the pounding as the lights fade the stage into darkness.*
6   *After a moment, the light come up on the SINGERS — soft, subdued*
7   *night colors. They sing a song that connects Christmas with Jesus*
8   *the Savior at Easter. [The original production used "Did Mary*
9   *Know?" by Richard Averre.] At the close of the song, bells can be*
10   *heard ringing around the hall. It's the KNAVES, all ringing hand*
11   *bells.)*
12   **KNAVE ONE:**   **Ring the bells and trumpets shout!**
13   **Our God has let the secret out!**
14   **KNAVE TWO:**   **Salvation shines in a corner not!**
15   **But leaps and laughs like the lame from their cots!**
16   **KNAVE THREE:**   **So let us call for the lights and sing!**
17   **For today is born a newborn King!**
18   *(Everyone cheers. The lights on the platform come up full. The*
19   *SINGERS begin to sing. Suggested song — "To Us Is Born*
20   *Immanuel." The CHOIR DIRECTOR turns to the congregation*
21   *and bids them join the SINGERS in "Hark! the Herald Angels Sing.")*
22   *SONG:*   "Hark! the Herald Angels Sing."
23   **SINGERS and CONGREGATION:**   *(Singing)* **Hark! the herald**
24   **angels sing,**
25   **"Glory to the newborn King:**
26   **Peace on earth, and mercy mild,**
27   **God and sinners reconciled!"**
28
29   **Joyful, all ye nations rise,**
30   **Join the triumph of the skies;**
31   **With th'angelic host proclaim,**
32   **"Christ is born in Bethlehem!"**
33
34   **Hark! the herald angels sing,**
35   **"Glory to the newborn King."**

1   **Christ, by highest heaven adored;**
2   **Christ, the everlasting Lord!**
3   **Late in time behold him come,**
4   **Offspring of the Virgin's womb.**
5
6   **Veiled in flesh the Godhead see;**
7   **Hail th'Incarnate Deity,**
8   **Pleased as man with men to dwell,**
9   **Jesus, our Emmanuel!**
10
11   **Hark! the herald angels sing,**
12   **"Glory to the newborn King."**
13
14   **Hail the heaven-born Prince of Peace!**
15   **Hail the Sun of Righteousness!**
16   **Light and life to all he brings,**
17   **Risen with healing in his wings.**
18
19   **Mild he lays his glory by,**
20   **Born that man no more may die;**
21   **Born to raise the sons of earth,**
22   **Born to give them second birth.**
23
24   **Hark! the herald angels sing,**
25   **"Glory to the newborn King!"**
26   *(At the close of the carol, the SINGERS sit around the platform.*
27   *The lights go to night colors. In the semidarkness, the SINGERS*
28   *become SHEEP and begin bleating, low and quietly. KNAVE*
29   *TWO and KNAVE THREE [playing the shepherds] come in,*
30   *herding the "sheep" around them. They wear shepherds' robes*
31   *or headpieces with ties. One of them is carrying a crate. They're*
32   *clearly not happy with their job.*
33   *(The SINGERS begin to make other animal sounds — cows,*
34   *horses, pigs . . . maybe even toucans. The KNAVES look at each*
35   *other quizzically. They flash a look at the SINGERS — who go*

33

1   *back to bleating softly. The KNAVES look at each other. They*
2   *shrug and put the crate down. KNAVE THREE steps in a sheep's*
3   *little "present" and winces. He wipes his sandal off on the*
4   *crate. He turns and snarls at the SHEEP. The SHEEP bleats*
5   *innocently.)*

6 **KNAVE THREE:** **And there —** *(Suddenly the SHEEP are*
7   *"baa-ing" loudly. The KNAVES shoot them a "Do you mind?"*
8   *look. The SHEEP fall silent.)* **And there were —** *(The SHEEP*
9   *"baa" again. The KNAVES flash them another look. The SHEEP*
10   *quiet down.)* **And there were —** *(Both KNAVES look back at*
11   *the SHEEP, waiting for the "baa-ing." The SHEEP smile back*
12   *guilelessly.)* **In the same country shepherds —** *(The SHEEP*
13   *jump in with their "baas." The KNAVES throw their arms up*
14   *in disgust.)*

15 **KNAVE TWO:** **Give us a break-eth!**

16 **KNAVE THREE:** *(Showing his fist)* **Lamb chops! Need-eth I say**
17   **more . . . ?** *(The SHEEP all nod their heads "no" with a*
18   *"baaah.")* **And there were in the same country shepherds**
19   **abiding in the field, and keeping watch over their flocks**
20   **by night.** *(The KNAVES stand around the box as if it were a*
21   *campfire. They rub their hands and roast their rears trying to*
22   *get warm. KNAVE TWO is humming "Angels We Have Heard*
23   *on High.")* **Hail, Frank.**

24 **KNAVE TWO:** **Evenin', Ernie.**

25 **KNAVE THREE:** **By my troth, 'tis a cold one.**

26 **KNAVE TWO:** **Indeed, I freezeth my —** *(Suddenly a bright*
27   *spotlight hits them both. There is a blast of music. The KNAVES*
28   *look up, terrified.)*

29 **ALL KNAVES:** *Whoooa-eth!*

30 **KNAVE TWO:** **And lo! An angel of the Lord came upon them.**

31 **KNAVE THREE:** **And the glory of the Lord shone round**
32   **about them!**

33 **KNAVE TWO:** **And they were sore afraid!** *(The KNAVES grab*
34   *onto each other in terror. Then they jump apart.)*

35 **ALL KNAVES:** *Ow!*

1   **KNAVE THREE:**   And the angel said unto them: *(KNAVE TWO*
2   *jumps up on the crate.)*
3   **KNAVE TWO:**   *(Proclaiming)* **"Fear not . . . *boys!* For behold I**
4   **bring you good tidings of great joy, which shall be to all**
5   **people. For unto you is born this day in the City of David**
6   **a savior, which is Christ the Lord. And this shall be a**
7   **sign unto you: Ye shall find the babe wrapped in**
8   **swaddling clothes and lying a manger!"** *(The SINGERS get*
9   *to their feet, holding a note that swells in intensity. The KNAVES*
10   *look around the sky.)*
11   **KNAVE THREE:**   **And suddenly there was with the angel a**
12   **multitude of the heavenly host praising God and saying,**
13   **"Glory to God in the highest, and on earth peace, good**
14   **will toward men."** *(The KNAVES stare up into the sky. The*
15   *SINGERS abruptly stop the note, and the bright spotlight fades.*
16   *KNAVE TWO steps down off the crate, eyes still glued to the*
17   *heavens.)* **And it came to pass, as the angels were gone**
18   **away from them into heaven, the shepherds said one to**
19   **the other —**
20   **KNAVE TWO:**   *Whoooah!*
21   **KNAVE THREE:**   *(Giving him a look)* **The shepherds said to one**
22   **another . . . ?**
23   **KNAVE TWO:**   **Oh . . . ah, "Let us now go even unto Bethlehem**
24   **and see this thing which is come to pass, which the Lord**
25   **hath made known to us." Right?** *(KNAVE THREE nods,*
26   *then grabs KNAVE TWO and pulls him toward the "manger."*
27   *They kneel in awe.)*
28   **KNAVE THREE:**   And they came with haste, and found Mary,
29   **and Joseph, and the babe lying in a manger.** *(As they stare*
30   *in amazement, the musical intro for "While By My Sheep" begins.*
31   *KNAVE THREE jumps up and strides into the aisles.)* **And**
32   **when they had seen it, they made abroad the saying**
33   **which was told them concerning this child. And all that**
34   **heard it wondered at those things which were told them**
35   **by the shepherds.**

1   **KNAVE TWO:** *(Still kneeling)* **But Mary kept all these things,**
2   **and pondered them in her heart.** *(Pauses a moment, then*
3   *he jumps up and joins KNAVE THREE.)* **And the shepherds**
4   **returned, glorifying and praising God for all the things**
5   **that they had heard and seen —**
6   **KNAVE THREE:**   **Which happened!**
7   **KNAVE TWO:**   **As it had been told unto them!** *(The KNAVES*
8   *lock arms around the shoulders and stride down the aisle.)*
9   **KNAVE THREE:**   **The weirdest things happen on the grave-**
10   **yard shift-eth.**
11   **KNAVE TWO:**   **Indeed-eth.**
12   **KNAVE THREE:**   **I wonderest what the boss will say regarding**
13   **angels and a manger?**
14   **KNAVE TWO:**   **Or about us leaving the sheep unattended to**
15   **go into town?** *(The KNAVES look at each other, wide-eyed.*
16   *Then they bolt down the aisle and out of the hall. The SINGERS*
17   *sing "While By My Sheep.")*
18   *SONG:*   "While By My Sheep."
19   **SINGERS:** *(Singing)* **While by my sheep I watch'd at night**
20   **Glad tidings brought an angel bright;**
21
22   **How great my joy! Joy, joy, joy!**
23   **Praise we the Lord in heav'n on high.**
24   **Praise we the Lord in heav'n on high.**
25
26   **There shall be born, so did he say,**
27   **In Bethlehem a child today.**
28
29   **How great my joy! Joy, joy, joy!**
30   **Praise we the Lord in heav'n on high.**
31   **Praise we the Lord in heav'n on high.**
32
33   **There shall he lie in a manger mean,**
34   **Who shall redeem the world from sin.**
35

1   How great my joy! Joy, joy, joy!

2   Praise we the Lord in heav'n on high.

3   Praise we the Lord in heav'n on high.

4

5   Lord, evermore to me be nigh,

6   Then shall my heart be fill'd with joy!

7

8   How great my joy! Joy, joy, joy!

9   Praise we the Lord in heav'n on high.

10   Praise we the Lord in heav'n on high.

11   *(This is followed with "The Coming of Our King" [or another*

12   *song that introduces the wise men].)*

13   **SONG:**   "The Coming of Our King."

14   **SINGERS:**   *(Singing)* **Hark, do you hear how the angel voices**

15   **sing?**

16   Bearing the news of the coming of a King.

17   Hark, do you hear how the angel voices sing?

18   Bearing the news of the coming of a King.

19

20   Jesus Christ is born to save us.

21   Satan's power no more enslaves us.

22   Hark, do you hear how the angel voices sing?

23   Bearing the news of the coming of a King!

24

25   See now a star shining in the Eastern skies

26   Guiding the wise men to where the infant lies.

27   See now a star shining in the Eastern skies

28   Guiding the wise men to where the infant lies.

29

30   Gifts they bring of all great treasure

31   Offer all they have without measure.

32   See now a star shining in the Eastern skies

33   Guiding the wise men to where the infant lies.

34

35   Come with the wise men, your faithful homage pay,

1	**Sing and rejoice that our Lord is born today,**
2	**Come with the wise men, your faithful homage pay,**
3	**Sing and rejoice that our Lord is born today.**
4	
5	**Greet the child with shouts of gladness,**
6	**Banish sorrow, banish all sadness.**
7	**Come with the wise men, your faithful homage pay,**
8	**Sing and rejoice that our Lord is born today.**
9	*(A SOLOIST steps forward and sings the first verse of "We Three*
10	*Kings." As he does, the KNAVES process down the center aisle,*
11	*wearing royal robes [no doubt lifted from the KING's armoire]*
12	*and obvious paper crowns. They are now the wise men, portrayed*
13	*more as the kings of medieval thinking than Magi.)*
14	*SONG:* "We Three Kings."
15	SOLOIST: *(Singing)* **We three kings of Orient are,**
16	**Bearing gifts we traverse afar**
17	**Field and fountain, moor and mountain,**
18	**Following yonder star.**
19	
20	**O star of wonder, star of night,**
21	**Star with royal beauty bright,**
22	**Westward leading, still proceeding,**
23	**Guide us to thy perfect light.**
24	*(At the top of the aisle, KNAVE TWO stops the other KNAVES.*
25	*He takes a breath and comes before the KING and QUEEN.*
26	*KNAVE TWO bows before them — and removes his paper crown.*
27	*He beckons toward the KING's crown.)*
28	**KNAVE TWO: If I might, my liege.** *(There are gasps from the*
29	*SINGERS. KNAVE ONE and KNAVE THREE look at each*
30	*other, astonished. The stunned KING looks at the QUEEN, who*
31	*smiles and nods. The KING sighs and takes off the crown. He*
32	*looks at it a moment, then extends it to KNAVE TWO, who takes*
33	*the crown and goes toward the congregation, holding the crown*
34	*in awe. He carefully lifts it up to his head and puts it on. More*
35	*gasps all around. KNAVE TWO enjoys the crown a moment,*

then turns to the KING and QUEEN.) **The crown means naught, if the knees will not bend.** *(KNAVE TWO lets this bold statement settle in, then turns to the congregation.)*

In my country, my crown means full much. Its brilliance compels fear and wonder. It forceth the bowed head and the open palm. It demandeth all reverence, and it is a jealous metal. It will receive none but all due. *(Pauses.)* **But this diadem is not mine. It belongeth to another.** *(He touches the crown for a moment, then takes it off and holds it out.)*

I felt the dire weight of that truth when I crooked my knee on Bethlehem's soil. We came to worship a child King. I brought gold as my homage. I thought it befitting the birth of one who maketh the stars find fearful new courses. *(He nods to KNAVE ONE and KNAVE THREE.)*

My fellows, caught together in the same strange journey, brought frankincense and myrrh. But these were temporal treasures: easily won, easily carried, easily laid at his cradle-throne. I knew then what this child desired was none less than this. *(He holds out the crown.)* **With the heart suspended within.** *(Pauses a moment, then he puts the crown on again.)*

When I rose and took my leave of Judea, I found the crown rode lighter upon this brow. Lighter because the Bethlehem child had taken the weight of it upon him. 'Twas no longer mine alone. I knew right well the man that wore this had become the loyal servant of a King. *(Pauses.)* **The crown means naught, if the knees will not bend.** *(KNAVE TWO turns to the KING and QUEEN. They are moved by his words, as are all the SINGERS. KNAVE TWO holds the crown out to the KING. The KING takes it and holds it a moment. He looks at KNAVE TWO.)*

KING: I thank thee, friend. *(The KING puts the crown back on his own head. KNAVE TWO bows. He goes out to the other KNAVES. They turn to the congregation.)*

KNAVE ONE: **There is much to astound us at this festive time.**

1   **KNAVE TWO:**   The angels, the wise men, the star as a sign.

2   **KNAVE THREE:**   But there is amazement above these to set

3   **this day apart.**

4   **KNAVE ONE:**   The baby born King can reign in our hearts.

5   *(The KNAVES process out of the hall. As the KNAVES go, a*

6   *SOLO VOICE begins "Joy to the World!" Soon all the SINGERS*

7   *are singing the carol.)*

8   *SONG:*   "Joy to the World!"

9   **SINGERS:** *(Singing)* **Joy to the world! the Lord is come:**

10   **Let earth receive her King;**

11   **Let every heart prepare him room,**

12   **And heaven and nature sing,**

13   **And heaven and nature sing,**

14   **And heaven, and heaven and nature sing.**

15

16   **Joy to the world! the Savior reigns:**

17   **Let men their songs employ;**

18   **While fields and floods, rocks, hills, and plains,**

19   **Repeat the sounding joy,**

20   **Repeat the sounding joy,**

21   **Repeat, repeat the sounding joy.**

22

23   **No more let sins and sorrows grow,**

24   **Nor thorns infest the ground;**

25   **He comes to make his blessings flow**

26   **Far as the curse is found,**

27   **Far as the curse is found,**

28   **Far as, far as the curse is found.**

29

30   **He rules the world with truth and grace,**

31   **And makes the nations prove**

32   **The glories of his righteousness,**

33   **And wonders of his love,**

34   **And wonders of his love,**

35   **And wonders, wonders of his love.**

1 **SCENE FOUR**
2 "Carols and Benedictions"
3
4 *(At the close of "Joy to the World!", the KING rises and faces*
5 *the congregation. He is obviously a new man, full of the season.)*
6 **KING:** **Let us with carols fill this place.**
7 **Good Choir Mistress (Master), lead us now with joyous pace!**
8 *(The CHOIR DIRECTOR bows and comes Downstage. She/he*
9 *can bid the congregation to stand and begin them in a carol sing*
10 *of familiar Christmas carols, ending with "Silent Night." At the*
11 *end of "Silent Night," the lights have gone to somber and*
12 *shadowy. The KNAVES come in from different directions. They*
13 *face the congregation.)*
14 **KNAVE ONE:** **I salute you. There is nothing I can give you**
15 **which you have not. But there is much, that while I**
16 **cannot give, you can take.**
17 **KNAVE TWO:** **No heaven can come to us, unless our hearts**
18 **find rest in it today. Take heaven.**
19 **KNAVE THREE:** **No peace lies in the future, which is not**
20 **hidden in this present instant. Take peace.**
21 **KNAVE TWO:** **The gloom of this world is but a shadow.**
22 **Behind it, yet within our reach, is joy. Take joy.**
23 **KNAVE ONE:** **And so, at this Christmas time, I greet you with**
24 **the prayer that for you, now and forever, the day breaks**
25 **and the shadows flee away.** *(Pause a moment, and the lights*
26 *come up full.)*
27 **EVERYONE:** ***Merry Christmas!*** *(Much cheering and applauding.*
28 *The SINGERS begin singing "We Wish You a Merry Christmas."*
29 *The KNAVES bow to the KING and QUEEN and dash out of*
30 *the hall.*
31 *(The SINGERS move out into the congregation, bowing to*
32 *the KING and QUEEN in small groups. Finally, the PAGES*
33 *with the banners march in followed by the JUGGLERS. They*
34 *bow to the KING and QUEEN. The KING and QUEEN rise and*
35 *process, smiling and waving at the congregation as they leave*

41

1   *the sanctuary. The PAGES and JUGGLERS follow the royal*

2   *couple out.)*

3   ***SONG:*** "We Wish You a Merry Christmas."

4   **SINGERS:** (Singing) **We wish you a merry Christmas,**

5   **We wish you a merry Christmas,**

6   **We wish you a merry Christmas,**

7   **And a happy new year!**

8

9   **Good tidings we bring**

10   **To you and your kin**

11   **Good tidings for Christmas**

12   **And a happy new year!**

13

14   **We wish you a merry Christmas,**

15   **We wish you a merry Christmas,**

16   **We wish you a merry Christmas,**

17   **And a happy new year!**

18

19   **Now bring us the figgy pudding,**

20   **Now bring us the figgy pudding,**

21   **Now bring us the figgy pudding,**

22   **And bring some right here!**

23

24   **We wish you a merry Christmas,**

25   **We wish you a merry Christmas,**

26   **We wish you a merry Christmas,**

27   **And a happy new year!**

28

29   **For we all love our figgy pudding,**

30   **We all love our figgy pudding,**

31   **We all love our figgy pudding,**

32   **So bring some out here!**

33

34   **And we won't go until we get some,**

35   **We won't go until we get some,**

1 **We won't go until we get some,**
2 **So bring some out here!**
3
4 **We wish you a merry Christmas,**
5 **We wish you a merry Christmas,**
6 **We wish you a merry Christmas,**
7 **And a happy new year!**
8 *(The SINGERS can finish the song at the back of the hall or*
9 *from the lobby.)*
10
11
12
13
14
15
16
17
18
19
20
21
22
23
24
25
26
27
28
29
30
31
32
33
34
35

THE WISE MEN HAD IT EASY

A Christmas
Shopping Musical

L. G. Enscoe
Annie Enscoe

Photo: Jeff Firestone Photography

A scene from the Fremont Mission Springs Community Church production of *The Wise Men Had it Easy.*

THE WISE MEN HAD IT EASY

CAST

SINGERS
(Singers 1-4 have speaking parts.)
DIRECTOR
CHOIR DIRECTOR
PASTOR
SHOPPER ONE
SHOPPER TWO
SHOPPER THREE
SALESMAN
FUNNY GUY ONE
FUNNY GUY TWO
KID WITH A BALLOON
KID ONE
KID TWO
CHILDREN'S CHOIR
AUDIENCE MEMBER ONE
AUDIENCE MEMBER TWO
AUDIENCE MEMBER THREE

PRODUCTION NOTES

Running Time

Seventy-five to eighty minutes.

Props

Mall sign; benches; potted plants; shopping bags; wrapped gifts; salesman gag props — several dollar bills, a book with *The Wise Man's Guide to Creative Christmas Financing* lettered on the front, and several booklets stuffed inside; funny guy gag props; Christmas lists with items crossed out that have been taped together and crumpled up (enough for all the Singers and Shoppers); check-out counter; wireless stereo headset; wallet with charge card; miscellaneous gift merchandise.

Costumes

The Singers and the Actors are dressed in wintery jewel-tone clothes. It should look as much like a Perry Como special as possible.

The Choir Director should be dressed very casually. The original production used a sweatshirt and jeans.

Shoppers One, Two and Three had matching turtlenecks and slacks or dresses. The Salesman is dressed as tacky as possible.

Set

The sanctuary is set to resemble a shopping mall. We accomplished this in the original production by using huge shopping bags down the sides of the sanctuary with department store names on them. The platform was suggestive of a mall concourse.

You can accomplish the same effect by hanging huge signs for SEARS, NORDSTROMS, MACY'S, etc. all over the sanctuary, along with benches with potted plants and a sign that says "Such-and-Such Mall." We also made the risers look like cement steps. The Singers carrying shopping bags also help create the geographical illusion.

Include a large, decorated Christmas tree in the scene. (The lights are not plugged in until later in the program.)

SUGGESTED MUSIC SOURCES

"It's the Most Wonderful Time of the Year," E. Pola and G. Wyle, arr. Hawley Ades, Shawnee Press.

"Silver Bells," Jay Livingston and Ray Evans, G & W Paramount Music.

"Carol of the Bells," M. Leontovich and Peter J. Willhousky, C. Fischer Music.

"Shopping," from a collection called *The Busy Side of Christmas,* Rick Powell, Temple Music Publishers.

"Sing the Joys of Christmas Near," Beth Thliveris, Gentry Publications.

"'Twas the Night Before Christmas," Clement Clark Moore; arr. Harry Simeone, Shawnee Press.

"Have Yourself a Merry Little Christmas," Hugh Martin and Ralph Blane, Loew's Inc./Leo Feist, Inc.

"Let It Snow!," Sammy Cahn and Jule Styne, Warner Bros. Music.

"Jingle Bells," Gordon Langford, Hinshaw Music.

"Winter Wonderland," Felix Bernard and Richard Smith; Warner Bros. Music or CPP Belwin.

"Wrap It All Up" by Mary Rice Hopkins, Big Steps Ministries, P.O. Box 362, Montrose, CA 91021

"That's Gotta Be," David Williams, Tempo Music Publications.

"O Christmas Tree," *Christmas 100 Seasonal Favorites,* Hal Leonard Publishing Co.

"Christmas With You," Douglas E. Wagner, Heritage Music Press.

"The Very Best Time of Year," John Rutter, Hinshaw Music Co.

"Christmas Is a Feeling," Natalie Sleeth, Hinshaw Music Co.

"Where Is Christmas?" Jerry Jay, Alfred Publishing Co., Inc.

"O Little Town of Bethlehem," Kay Hawkes Goodyear, Chapel Hill Music.

"Angel's Carol," John Rutter, Hinshaw Music Co.

"One Small Babe," Jay Althouse, Hope Publishing Co.

"Lyllay My Liking," Gustav Holst, J. Curwen & Sons Ltd./G. Schirmer.

"Tomorrow Shall Be My Dancing Day," John Gardner, Oxford University Press.

"Mary's Little Boy Child," Jester Hairston, Schumann Music.

"Gloria! Gloria!" Mary E. Caldwell; Schmitt, Hall & McCreary.

"The Star Carol," Alfred S. Burt, Shawnee Press.

"We Wish You a Merry Christmas," arr. John Rutter, Hinshaw Music Co.

AUTHORS' NOTES

The Wise Men Had It Easy is a seriously comic look at the busiest season of all: Christmas.

The program is set in a mall, where a church choir is rehearsing after hours for a concert they plan to perform the next night. During the evening of light holiday tunes comes a trio of Shoppers whose stories eventually lead us to the real Gift of Christmas.

Lighting instructions are included. While lights enhance the drama, they are not necessary.

You can, of course, choose your own music for the program. The script suggests themes and tones with the song choices from the original production.

Make sure to keep the tone light at first, gradually folding in the serious themes in small, equal and then full measures.

God bless your work.

ACT ONE
"The Gifts Given"

*(The sanctuary is in darkness. A taped Muzak "Silent Night"
can be heard — a lush, sweet string version. This lasts a few
moments, then the taped sounds of a mall intrude over the top
of the music. We hear people shopping, Muzak, telephones, car
horns, cash registers, etc. The lights come up.)*

*(The sanctuary looks like a mall, with potted plants, huge depart-
ment store signs, benches, and freestanding billboards.*

*(The SINGERS [this is a multigenerational choir, now playing
SHOPPERS] break in from all around the sanctuary: the sides,
the aisles, and from the pews. They carry shopping bags from
major department stores and are all involved in little pantomime
vignettes: Some tug at tired children. Others argue over the price
of something. Ring up sales. Look through merchandise. All mall
kinds of activities. Lots of sound and fury.*

*(As the mall sounds fade out, the SINGERS break into song.
Suggested song: "It's the Most Wonderful Time of the Year." As
the SINGERS begin their next verse, the DIRECTOR comes in,
carrying a clipboard and wearing a wireless headset. He or she
watches the commotion, looking quite stressed.)*

**DIRECTOR: This isn't the way it's supposed to be, is it?!
What's going on here?! I'm looking for Christmas!** *(The
SINGERS sing a few more lines.)* **This isn't Christmas! Give
me Christmas! Stop! Everyone stop what you're doing!
Stooop!** *(The SINGERS stop and turn to the DIRECTOR.)* **What
are you doing? Does this look like Christmas to any of
you? Now, we rehearsed this opening five times. What is
the *problem*?** *(The SINGERS start talking among themselves,
arguing about what the problem may be.)*

     **People, people, listen up! The mall has graciously
given us this time after hours to rehearse for our Christmas concert here — which I don't think I need to remind
any of you is *tomorrow* night.** *(The SINGERS talk again,*

1   *complaining about not having enough time to learn music or*
2   *rehearse — the usual stuff.)*
3   **OK, OK. We're going to be fine. All right? We're going**
4   **to look just great. Let's talk about this opening, OK? I**
5   **said to you, "Come in singing and show me what**
6   **Christmas is all about."**
7   **SINGER ONE:**   **That's what we did!**
8   **DIRECTOR:**   **No, you gave me the blue-light special at K-Mart.**
9   **You gave me zero-shopping-days-left-shoppers. I want to**
10   **see big smiles, peace on earth, joy to the world!**
11   **SINGER TWO:**   **You ever been at this mall when it's open**
12   **during Christmas?**
13   **SINGER THREE:**   **I didn't see anybody smiling.**
14   **SINGER FOUR:**   **And not much joy to the world. Even when**
15   **they were playing it over the mall speakers.** *(The*
16   *SINGERS agree among themselves.)*
17   **DIRECTOR:**   **OK. Fine. Forget the opening. Let's go on with**
18   **the rest of the program, all right?** *(To the light booth)*
19   **Lights? We're moving on, OK?** *(The DIRECTOR turns to go,*
20   *sees the audience sitting there for the first time.)* **Wait a minute.**
21   **What are all of you doing here?**
22   **AUDIENCE MEMBER ONE:**   **We're waiting for the mall to**
23   **open!**
24   **DIRECTOR:**   **You're waiting for the mall to open . . . ? But the**
25   **mall doesn't open until tomorrow morning! That's . . .**
26   *(Checks watch)* **. . . twelve hours from now!**
27   **AUDIENCE MEMBER TWO:**   **We want to be first in line!**
28   **AUDIENCE MEMBER THREE:**   **I still have fifty-eight people**
29   **on my list!**
30   **DIRECTOR:**   *(To the SINGERS)* **I'm really sorry about this,**
31   **folks. They said the mall was going to be empty for our**
32   **rehearsal.** *(Turns to the audience.)* **OK. I'm sorry, but this**
33   **is a closed rehearsal. I'm afraid I'm going to have to ask**
34   **you all to wait outside —**
35   **SINGERS:**   *(Individuals shout out)* **No! It's OK! Let them stay!**

1   **We want to sing for them!** *(Etc.) (The DIRECTOR looks*
2   *irritated, then gives in.)*
3   **DIRECTOR: All right, all right! The audience can stay. But**
4   **then I want to make this like a *real* concert.** *(The PASTOR*
5   *walks into the playing area.)*
6   **PASTOR: Sorry, I'm a little late.**
7   **DIRECTOR: Pastor, great! I'm glad you're here. Would you**
8   **pray with us?**
9   **PASTOR: Be glad to.**
10   **DIRECTOR: OK. You've got...** *(Checks watch)* **...three**
11   **minutes.** *(The PASTOR grins at the DIRECTOR.)*
12   **PASTOR: OK, I'll make it snappy.** *(The PASTOR turns to the*
13   *audience and offers the greeting and prayer.)* **I'm glad you're**
14   **all with us. I'd like to welcome you here tonight. Would**
15   **you pray with me?** *(Or something like this.)*
16   *(After the PASTOR has finished, he/she says good-bye and leaves.*
17   *The DIRECTOR motions to the light booth. The lights come*
18   *down to a pool of winter evening colors. An ensemble comes*
19   *forward and sings a medley of secular Christmas tunes. [The*
20   *original production used "Evening in December" by Walda and*
21   *arranged by Maddux. When this is finished the lights come up*
22   *for the rest of the SINGERS to join the ensemble and sing a*
23   *secular Christmas song. Suggested song: "Silver Bells."*
24   *(The DIRECTOR signals the lights to take on a softer hue. The*
25   *SINGERS [or a smaller ensemble] move into a vocal arrangement*
26   *of a Christmas number. Suggested song: "Carol of the Bells."*
27   *When they are done, the WOMEN sing an upbeat holiday tune.*
28   *Suggested song: "Sing the Joys of Christmas Near." The*
29   *DIRECTOR comes toward the SINGERS with a big smile.)*
30   **DIRECTOR: Well. You sing like that when there's an**
31   **audience and we'll be all right.** *(Looks at the audience.)* **I**
32   **mean, a *real* audience. Anyway, choir? We have to work**
33   **out some light cues for a few minutes. We want to make**
34   **sure everyone can see you — not like last year. Why don't**
35   **you take a break?** *(The SINGERS talk among themselves and*

1   *sit. The lights come down on the SINGERS.)* **OK, that's great.**
2   *(If using lights, to the light booth)* **Let's work on that last**
3   **cue.** *(Turns to go. Sees the audience again. Looks at his or her*
4   *watch.)* **Eleven hours and twenty minutes.** *(The DIRECTOR*
5   *goes up the aisle. The SINGERS talk among themselves for a*
6   *moment. Then SHOPPER ONE comes toward the stage out of*
7   *the audience, carrying a mall shopping bag. He or she steps in*
8   *front of the SINGERS, who all suddenly notice and stop talking*
9   *to listen.)*
10 SHOPPER ONE: **Busy sidewalks, shoppers rushing home**
11   **with their treasures, happiest time of the year. Fun songs.**
12   **But I was here at the mall today. Let me be a witness. It**
13   **was not fun. Yes, I survived the inevitable today. I. Went.**
14   **Shopping. Here's the proof.** *(She pulls out a crumpled, taped*
15   *up, crossed out Christmas list.)* **Does this look familiar to**
16   **anyone here? "The List." Look at it. It's been folded,**
17   **spindled and mutilated. It's been torn up, taped together,**
18   **and cried on. Am I the only one?** *(SHOPPER TWO and*
19   *SHOPPER THREE come up from the audience. They're waving*
20   *similar lists. They show them to each other and laugh.)*
21 SHOPPER TWO: *(Writing on the back of a list)* **Wait a minute**
22   **here. I wanna start another list. It's called, "How Many**
23   **Times I've Forgotten It Was Christmas." Lemme see. Well,**
24   **there were the five times I double-parked . . . and the two**
25   **times I triple-parked . . . and then there are those words**
26   **I used when I got the parking tickets . . . Oh, yes, and**
27   **then there's that angelic moment when I parked in the**
28   **handicapped zone and limped into the store.**
29 SHOPPER THREE: **I'll do you one better. This was** *me* **today.**
30   *(Suddenly turns and shouts Off-stage:)* **"Don't give me that**
31   **look! That parking space was** *mine,* **buddy! Get over it — I**
32   **saw it first! Yeah-huh! I spotted it when I was coming**
33   **around Montgomery Ward two blocks away! Yeah, well**
34   **merry Christmas to you.** *I* **had to park in the J. C. Penney**
35   **loading dock."** *(Looks the other way.)* **"Hey, wait! Wait a**

1   minute! That's my car! Hey, pal! OK, make nice and put
2   away the forklift!"
3 SHOPPER ONE: I was going up the eleventy billionth
4   escalator today, and I was looking at all the decorations.
5   All the numb faces. All the shopping bags all clutched
6   and overstuffed . . . and I started getting this . . . I don't
7   know, you wouldn't call it déjà vu. That's where you think
8   you've been there before, but you don't know when. What
9   do you call it when you know you've been there before,
10   but you don't know why you even bother?
11 SHOPPER THREE: That's called déjà fooey.
12 SHOPPER TWO: All I can remember is . . . "Gift wrap is on
13   the fourth floor."
14 SHOPPER THREE: "I'm sorry, I'm all out of boxes for this
15   item."
16 SHOPPER ONE: "Will that be Visa? American Express?
17   MasterCard? Traveler's checks? Discover? Layaway?
18   ATM card? Firstborn child?"
19 SHOPPER TWO: "Is this supposed to be for a man or
20   woman?"
21 SHOPPER THREE: "I'm sorry, I'm all out of tissue for this
22   item."
23 SHOPPER TWO: *(To a "child")* "Just eight or nine more hours,
24   honey, then we can go home."
25 SHOPPER THREE: "I'm sorry . . . I'm all out of this item."
26 SHOPPER ONE: *(Announcer voice)* "Attention, shoppers. The
27   store will be closing in five minutes!"
28 SHOPPERS TWO and THREE: *Nooo!*
29 SHOPPER ONE: *(Announcer voice)* Merry Christmas, shoppers!
30   *(Small pause. The SHOPPERS holds up their lists.)*
31 ALL SHOPPERS: The wise men had it easy. They only had to
32   buy for one.
33   *(Blackout. In the darkness, we hear the sound of shopping*
34   *again — the same sounds that opened the program. The lights*
35   *come up. The SINGERS are doing their shopping pantomimes*

1   *again. They sing a song about shopping. This should be a*
2   *humorous song about the stress of buying gifts. [The original*
3   *production used "Shopping" by Powell.] In the middle of the*
4   *song, while the music still continues, the SHOPPERS rush back*
5   *On-stage, vaudeville style.)*

6   **SHOPPER ONE:** *(Showing list)* **One more person!**

7   **SHOPPER TWO:** *(Showing list)* **Eight more people!**

8   **SHOPPER THREE:** **Twenty-two more people!**

9   **SHOPPERS ONE and TWO:** *What?!*

10   **SHOPPER THREE:** **I just started tonight.**

11   **SHOPPER ONE:** **But the store's closing in five minutes!**

12   **SHOPPER TWO:** **And it's Christmas Eve!**

13   **SHOPPER ONE:** **What're you gonna do?**

14   **SHOPPER THREE:** **Hey, isn't Seven-Eleven open all night?**

15   **SHOPPER TWO:** **You're right!**

16   **SHOPPER ONE:** **Can they gift-wrap a Slurpie?**

17   **SHOPPER THREE:** **Worth a try! Come on!** *(The SHOPPERS*
18   *stop and look at the audience.)*

19   **ALL SHOPPERS:** **The wise men had it easy. They only had**
20   **to buy for one.** *(The SHOPPERS exit. The SINGERS continue*
21   *their shopping song. When the song is finished, the lights come*
22   *down on the SINGERS and a spotlight comes up downstage.*
23   *SALESMAN enters. He's dressed like a tacky pitchman and*
24   *holds up several items.)*

25   **SALESMAN:** **You try red. You try blue. You even try those**
26   **jewel tones like . . . cranberry and cinnamon. But there's**
27   **no way around it, folks!** *(He holds out a bunch of dollar bills.)*
28   **You can't celebrate Christmas without the green!**
29   *(He laughs.)* **Oh, come on now! You know you love presents.**
30   **And when you come up empty-handed with a friend who**
31   **hands you a measly Christmas card — don't you try and**
32   **give anyone that old "You know it's the thought that**
33   **counts" routine! We all know that's just another way of**
34   **saying, "You cheap weasel! Just see what I get *you* next**
35   **year!" Well, folks! Now you'll never have to sweat another**

1   Christmas. Not with . . . *(He holds up a book.)*
2   *Wise Man's Guide to Creative Christmas Financing!*
3   Look what you get! First there's a nifty guide that gets
4   your hands on those quickie money sources, like second
5   mortgages, life insurance policies and children's college
6   savings.
7   And you'll also find wonderful inspirational gift-
8   buying chapters, like "Who Needs the Manger When You
9   Need the Manager," "Celebrity Gift Ideas," and "Buying
10   Love With Presents That Work."
11   You'll also discover handy credit information,
12   including quick applications for over three dozen credit
13   cards that ask *no* questions. *(He pulls out booklets.)* Plus
14   you'll get these handy booklets, such as "Raising Your
15   Credit Limits and Your Self-Esteem" and "How to Put
16   the Bank Back in Bankruptcy" complete with IRS
17   applications. Call now for this amazing offer. Remember
18   our motto: "What's Christmas Without the Green?" Merry
19   Christmas, everyone! *(The spotlight goes out. The SINGERS*
20   *are talking among themselves, laughing at what they just saw.*
21   *Then some of them look up. The DIRECTOR is standing there,*
22   *looking at them oddly.)*
23 DIRECTOR: Boy, you people sure have a lot of energy
24   tonight. What's so funny? *(The SINGERS look at each*
25   *other and shrug innocently.)* Just love to rehearse, huh?
26   What troopers. OK, I need to work with the light people
27   a few more minutes. Let me see . . . *(Calls names of*
28   *SINGERS in a quartet or quintet)* . . . why don't you guys
29   work on *(Name of song here)*. OK? I'll be back in a few
30   minutes. *(The DIRECTOR starts up the aisle. The lights come*
31   *up on a quartet or quintet. The DIRECTOR looks back, then up*
32   *at the light booth.)* Well, you guys got *one* light cue right
33   tonight! *(The DIRECTOR goes out of the sanctuary. The quartet*
34   *or quintet begins singing another song about the gift-buying*
35   *season.*

1   *(At the end of the song, two FUNNY GUYS sneak onto the stage.*
2   *They're carrying shopping bags. The SINGERS look at them with*
3   *grins.)*
4   **FUNNY GUY ONE:** *(To the SINGERS, quietly)* **Hey, any'a you**
5   **guys know "'Twas the Night Before Christmas"?** *(The*
6   *SINGERS grin, nod and quietly break up into their positions for*
7   *the song, looking around to see if the DIRECTOR is watching.*
8   *Suggested song: "'Twas the Night Before Christmas." If you do not*
9   *wish to use the musical version, the SINGERS may perform the*
10   *poem as a Readers Theatre.)*
11   **FUNNY GUY TWO: Great. *Hit it!***
12   *SONG:* "'Twas the Night Before Christmas." *(As the song or*
13   *reading happens, the FUNNY GUYS do a pantomime routine,*
14   *acting out Mom, Dad, Sugar Plums, Santa, Reindeer, etc. There*
15   *are lots of sight gags: Detergent boxes for "Dash away, dash away,*
16   *dash away — All!" "Dad" hands "Mom" a used kerchief to wear*
17   *while he puts on a tacky cap. A toy Santa and Reindeer can be used*
18   *for "miniature sleigh and eight tiny reindeer." Stage devices for the*
19   *sound effects in the song: "clatter, whistled," etc. Also, fun make-up*
20   *can be slapped on the actor playing Santa during the "nose like a*
21   *cherry" verses.)*
22   **SINGERS: 'Twas the night before Christmas**
23   **And all through the house,**
24   **Not a creature was stirring,**
25   **Not even a mouse.**
26
27   **The stockings were hung**
28   **By the chimney with care,**
29   **In hopes that St. Nicholas**
30   **Soon would be there.**
31
32   **The children were nestled**
33   **All snug in their wee little beds,**
34   **While visions of sugar plums**
35   **Danced in their wee little heads.**

1   Mama in her kerchief,
2   And I in my cap,
3   Had just settled down
4   For a long winter's nap.
5

6   When out on the lawn
7   There arose such a clatter,
8   I sprang from my bed
9   To see what was the matter.
10

11   Away to the window
12   I flew like a flash,
13   Tore open the shutters,
14   Threw open the sash.
15

16   What to my wondering
17   Eyes should appear,
18   But a miniature sleigh,
19   And eight tiny reindeer.
20

21   With a little old driver,
22   So lively and quick,
23   That I knew right away,
24   That it must be St. Nick.
25

26   More rapid than eagles
27   His coursers they came,
28   And he whistled and shouted,
29   And called them by name;
30

31   "Now Dasher! Now Dancer!
32   Now Prancer! Now Vixen!
33   On Comet! On Cupid!
34   On Donner and Blitzen!
35

1	To the top of the porch,
2	To the top of the wall!
3	Dash away, dash away,
4	Dash away all!"
5	
6	So up to the housetops
7	The coursers they flew,
8	With a sleigh full of toys,
9	And St. Nicholas, too.
10	
11	And then in a twinkling,
12	I heard on the roof
13	All the clattering
14	Of each galloping hoof.
15	
16	All bundled in fur,
17	From his head to his foot;
18	His clothes were all tarnished
19	With ashes and soot.
20	
21	I drew in my head
22	And was turning around,
23	When down the chimney
24	He came with a bound.
25	
26	A bag full of toys
27	He had flung on his back,
28	And he looked like a little old peddler
29	Just opening his pack.
30	
31	His eyes, how they twinkled so gay.
32	His dimples, how merry were they!
33	His cheeks were like roses
34	Kissed by the sun!
35	His nose like a cherry,

1   All wrinkled with fun!
2
3   His droll little mouth
4   Was drawn up like a bow!
5   The beard on his chin
6   Was whiter than snow.
7
8   The stump of a little old pipe
9   He held tight in his teeth,
10   And the smoke went around,
11   And around, and around, and around
12   His head like a wreath.
13
14   Oh! He was so jolly and plump,
15   A right, jolly old, jolly old elf.
16   And I laughed, and I laughed,
17   And I laughed when I saw him,
18   In spite of myself.
19
20   He had a broad face
21   And a little round belly
22   That shook while he laughed
23   Like a bowl full of jelly.
24
25   He gave me a wink of his eye,
26   And a twist of his head,
27   A chuckle and a smile,
28   I knew all the while,
29   I had nothing to dread.
30
31   He spoke not a word,
32   But went right to his work,
33   He filled all the stockings,
34   Then turned with a jerk.
35

1	And laying a finger
2	Aside of his nose
3	And giving a nod
4	Up the chimney he rose.
5	
6	He sprang to his sleigh,
7	To his team gave a whistle
8	And away they all flew
9	Like the down of a thistle.
10	
11	But I head him exclaim
12	'Ere he drove out of sight.
13	"Merry Christmas to all,
14	And to all a good night!"
15	
16	'Tis the night after Christmas
17	And all through the house,
18	Not a creature is stirring,
19	Not even a mouse.
20	
21	The presents are scattered
22	And broken, I fear.
23	And St. Nicholas won't come again
24	For a year.
25	
26	The children are nestled
27	All snug in their wee little beds,
28	While mem'ries of sugar plums
29	Dance in their wee little heads.
30	
31	Mama in her kerchief,
32	Papa in his cap,
33	Are settled down
34	For a long winter's nap.
35	*(The DIRECTOR walks on, arms crossed. The FUNNY GUYS*

1   *smile sheepishly, quickly gather up their props, throw them in*
2   *the bags, and are gone. The DIRECTOR turns to the audience.)*
3   **DIRECTOR:**   Uh . . . at this point in the program, you see, the
4   **audience is supposed to sing along with the choir. I don't**
5   **know, since you're all here for . . .** *(Checks his watch)*
6   **. . . eleven more hours, I thought you wouldn't mind**
7   **pretending you're a real audience for a little while and**
8   **joining in. You don't mind? You guys are great.** *(The*
9   *CHOIR DIRECTOR directs the choirs, audience [and soloists]*
10   *in a medley of secular Christmas carols. Suggested songs: "Have*
11   *Yourself a Merry Little Christmas," "Let It Snow!", "Jingle*
12   *Bells," "Walkin' in a Winter Wonderland."*
13   *(As the carols finish, the CHILDREN'S CHOIR comes in and*
14   *sits. A KID WITH A BALLOON sadly walks across the stage.*
15   *He stops Center Stage. KID ONE and KID TWO enter from*
16   *opposite sides of the playing area. They cross to Center Stage.)*
17   **KID ONE:**   *(A chant)* **Don't touch anything! Don't touch**
18   **anything! Don't touch anything!**
19   **KID TWO:**   *(A chant; same time)* **You wanna spanking? No! You**
20   **wanna spanking? No! You wanna spanking? No!** *(They stop*
21   *when they see the KID WITH A BALLOON.)*
22   **KID WITH A BALLOON:**   *(To KID ONE)* **What did your mother**
23   **say to you?**
24   **KID ONE:**   **She tol' me I better not touch nuthin' while she**
25   **was shoppin' or *nooo* Christmas.**
26   **KID WITH A BALLOON:**   *(To KID TWO)* **What did she say to**
27   **you?**
28   **KID TWO:**   **She said to stop cryin' or she'd really give me**
29   **somethin' to cry about.**
30   **KID WITH A BALLOON:**   **My mom told me if I wanted to live**
31   **to see Christmas, I better not make a peep.**
32   **KIDS ONE and TWO:**   **Did you?**
33   **KID WITH A BALLOON:**   **No way! And I had to peep all night!**
34   *(Pause)* **I hate shopping. Christmas isn't as fun as it used to be.**
35   **KIDS ONE and TWO:**   *(Nodding)* **Bogus.** *(The music begins for a*

1   *song by the CHILDREN'S CHOIR. The children come forward*

2   *and sing. [The original production used "Wrap It All Up" by*

3   *Mary Rice Hopkins.] At the close of the song, the lights spring*

4   *to life on the Christmas tree.)*

5 **KID ONE: You guys see that?!**

6 **KID TWO: That's awesome!**

7   *(The CHILDREN'S CHOIR runs to the tree and gathers around*

8   *it. The CHILDREN'S CHOIR and some members of the*

9   *SINGERS perform a fun song about Christmas trees. [The*

10   *original production used "That's Gotta Be (The Biggest*

11   *Christmas Tree)" by Williams.] At the conclusion of the song,*

12   *the MEN move down to the tree and sing, "O Christmas Tree.")*

13 *SONG:*   "O Christmas Tree."

14 **MEN SINGERS:** *(Singing)* **O Christmas tree, O Christmas tree,**

15   **How lovely are thy branches;**

16   **Not only green when summer's here,**

17   **But in the coldest time of year.**

18   **O Christmas tree, O Christmas tree,**

19   **How lovely are thy branches.**

20   *(During this carol, the CHILDREN'S CHOIR is exiting the sanctuary.)*

21   **O Christmas tree, O Christmas tree,**

22   **How richly God has decked thee.**

23   **Thou bidst us true and faithful be,**

24   **And trust in God unchangingly.**

25   **O Christmas tree, O Christmas tree,**

26   **How richly God has decked thee!**

27   *(The MEN rejoin the rest of the SINGERS. They talk among*

28   *themselves. The spotlight picks up a duet. They sing a warm*

29   *Christmas chestnut about snow and Christmas memories. [The*

30   *original production used "Christmas With You."] At the conclusion*

31   *of the song, a soloist can come forward and sing another tune about*

32   *the season. [The original production used a song written especially*

33   *for the evening.] When the song is done, a spotlight comes up on*

34   *SHOPPER TWO. He or she is standing in a check-out line with*

35   *a couple of items looking nervous and very tired.)*

1   **SHOPPER TWO:** *(To a "shopper")* **Are you next? Oh.** *(Turns to*
2   *the "clerk.")* **Guess I'm up.** *(Puts items on the counter.)* **I'm**
3   **glad you guys are open late. I don't know what I'd do.**
4   **I'm sure** *you* **don't like being open late. What? Oh, I'm**
5   **sorry.** *(Looks behind him.)* **Yeah, there** *are* **a lot of people**
6   **waiting. Sorry.** *(Opens a wallet.)* **I'm going to use my charge**
7   **card.** *(Hands the "clerk" a credit card. Then turns and looks at*
8   *the "person" behind him.)* **I always start shopping too late,**
9   **you know?** *(Hears something and looks back to the "clerk.")*
10   **Excuse me? What do you mean it won't take my card?**
11   **Oh, I gave you the expired one, didn't I? I'll just — what?**
12   **That's the right card? Then I don't understand why I —**
13   **wait, wait. Are you saying I can't buy these things? Of**
14   **course I can, just not with this card. No, I didn't bring**
15   **cash. I didn't bring my checkbook, either. I thought I'd**
16   **just charge — yes, I know. Not with this card. Look, I**
17   **mailed a payment, so I don't know why it's not letting**
18   **you — I don't know, a couple of days ago. Can you call**
19   **them and see if they've credited my account? Yes, I know**
20   **you're busy, but it's ten minutes till closing and I have**
21   **to get these things tonight. Please. Well, can I call them?**
22   **Let me talk to the manager. You're the manager? You're**
23   **sixteen years old! Eighteen, sorry. OK, tell me what I can**
24   **do. Make my payments on time. Well, thank you, I'll make**
25   **that my New Year's resolution.** *(Takes the card.)* **Can you**
26   **put these things back for me?** *(Turns away, fighting back*
27   *humiliation.)*
28   **I can't believe this. I made a payment. I was counting**
29   **on this card. I was** *counting* **on it. Well, that's it, isn't it?**
30   **No credit, no Christmas.** *(SHOPPER TWO starts to go, but*
31   *stops.)* **The wise men had it easy. They only had to buy**
32   **for one.** *(The spotlight fades on SHOPPER TWO. The lights*
33   *come up on the SINGERS. They sing a reflective Christmas song.*
34   *Suggested song: "The Very Best Time of the Year."*
35   *(The lights shift to cool hues, coming down very intimately on the*

1	*SINGERS or a soloist. A song is performed that wonders what*
2	*Christmas is supposed to mean. Suggested songs: "Where Is*
3	*Christmas?" and "Christmas Is a Feeling."*
4	*(The lights come down on the SINGERS. [The CHOIR*
5	*DIRECTOR seats them.] SHOPPER ONE wanders On-stage*
6	*from the audience, carrying a shopping bag. He or she looks*
7	*achingly weary and emotionally dragged out. At first he or she*
8	*talks to the SINGERS, then turns to the audience.)*
9	**SHOPPER ONE: I remember . . . I don't know . . . maybe I**
10	**was eight. Yes, I was eight. It was the year I got my Huffy**
11	**bike with the great banana seat. Anyway, I was eight and**
12	**it was Christmas Eve. I was in my room, counting the**
13	**hours. It was the only day all year I couldn't wait for it**
14	**to get dark so I could go to sleep. I knew that if I could**
15	**get myself to fall asleep, see, the morning would come in**
16	**a flash and it would be Christmas Day.**
17	**That's not the last time I've used sleep to get me**
18	**from Christmas Eve to Christmas Day. Anyway, I'm in**
19	**my room and I can hear crying. I know it's not the TV.**
20	**You can always tell crying on the TV. No, this is real**
21	**crying. It's my mother crying. Not loud. Just soft. And**
22	**not sniffles, like you get from a Kodak commercial. This**
23	**was crying from deep inside. Well, I panicked. Crying**
24	**and Christmas. They didn't go together. I got that sick,**
25	**tight feeling in my stomach. The kind you get when you**
26	**hear your mother giving in. Suddenly the world gets**
27	**scary for a moment. And I didn't know if I should hide**
28	**in my room or go see why . . . why my mother would be**
29	**crying on Christmas Eve. I opened the door quietly. So**
30	**she wouldn't hear me. If I could just see that she was just**
31	**crying over a Christmas card or the cookies not turning**
32	**out, then I could just sneak back to my room and she'd**
33	**never know I heard her.**
34	**I tiptoed down the hallway and peeked around the**
35	**kitchen wall . . . and, well, she was sitting at the table. She**

1   had a photo album in front of her. Maybe she's crying
2   over Grandmother; she'd died the year before. Maybe it
3   was pictures of Grams and it made her cry. That was a
4   good enough reason, so I started to creep back down the
5   hall. But she saw me. She wiped her face with a dish
6   towel. She called me toward her. But I froze. "The
7   pictures, Mom?" I said. "Are they makin' you cry?" She
8   shook her head. She looked down at the floor.
9   "It's gone." That's what she said. "It's gone." What
10   was gone? Her car keys? Her wedding ring? Her glasses?
11   "It's gone and I can't get it back. I don't know where I
12   put it. I thought I put it somewhere that I'd remember.
13   How could I lose Christmas?" How could she lose
14   *Christmas?* *I* could never lose Christmas. I never
15   understood what my mom meant. Never. In fact, I forgot
16   about it. Until tonight. Tonight I lost Christmas. No, that's
17   not it. Tonight I realized I never had it. All season. It's
18   gone. I wish it were just my car keys. Or my glasses. That
19   would be easy. *(Pauses.)* How do you get Christmas back?
20   *(The DIRECTOR, who has been listening, steps into the light.*
21   *He or she walks to SHOPPER ONE.)*
22   DIRECTOR: Are you OK?
23   SHOPPER ONE: *(Pulling it together)* Yes. Sure. I'll be fine.
24   *(Starts to go out, then stops.)* Oh . . . ah, I know you're
25   busy . . . but . . . could you — no, that's stupid. Never
26   mind.
27   DIRECTOR: What?
28   SHOPPER ONE: Could you . . . do you think you could sing
29   "O Little Town of Bethlehem"? That was my mother's
30   favorite.
31   DIRECTOR: Well, we're supposed to rehearse "White
32   Christmas." That's next on the program.
33   SHOPPER ONE: *(Slightly hurt)* Oh, that's OK. Thanks anyway.
34   *(SHOPPER ONE starts up the center aisle. One of the SINGERS*
35   *suddenly stands and starts singing the first verse of "O Little*

1   *Town of Bethlehem." SHOPPER ONE stops mid-aisle and*
2   *smiles. Turns and listens. The DIRECTOR nods and backs*
3   *away.)*
4   **SONG:**   "O Little Town of Bethlehem."
5   **SOLOIST ONE: O Little Town of Bethlehem!**
6   **How still we see thee lie,**
7   **Above thy deep and dreamless sleep**
8   **The silent stars go by;**
9   **Yet in thy dark streets shineth**
10   **The everlasting Light;**
11   **The hopes and fears**
12   **Of all the years**
13   **Are met in thee tonight.**
14   *(Another soloist picks up the second verse. And then another,*
15   *until finally all the SINGERS are standing and singing the*
16   *carol.)*
17   **SOLOIST TWO: For Christ is born of Mary,**
18   **And gathered all above,**
19   **While mortals sleep,**
20   **The angels keep**
21   **Their watch of wondering love.**
22   **O morning stars, together**
23   **Proclaim the holy birth!**
24   **And praises sing to God the King,**
25   **And peace to men on earth.**
26   **SOLOIST THREE: How silently, how silently,**
27   **The wondrous Gift is given!**
28   **So God imparts to human hearts**
29   **The blessings of his heaven.**
30   **No ear may hear his coming,**
31   **But in this world of sin,**
32   **Where meek souls will**
33   **Receive him still,**
34   **The dear Christ enters in.**
35   **SINGERS: O holy Child of Bethlehem!**

1   **Descend to us, we pray;**
2   **Cast out our sins, and enter in,**
3   **Be born in us today.**
4   **We hear the Christmas angels**
5   **The great glad tidings tell,**
6   **O come to us, abide with us;**
7   **Our Lord Emmanuel!**
8   *(At the close of the carol, SHOPPER ONE stands there a moment.*
9   *He or she has finally found Christmas.)*
10   **SHOPPER ONE:**   *(Smiling, whispering)* **Thank you.** *(SHOPPER*
11   *ONE exits down the center aisle.)*
12
13
14
15
16
17
18
19
20
21
22
23
24
25
26
27
28
29
30
31
32
33
34
35

1   **ACT TWO**

2   "The Gift Given"

3

4   *(The SINGERS are very moved by what has happened. The*

5   *CHOIR DIRECTOR leads them in a selection of sacred music.*

6   *This is staged as a mini-concert, shifting the tone of the program.*

7   *It can include any collection of, perhaps, less-familiar carols.*

8   *[The original production used "Angel's Carol" by John Rutter,*

9   *"One Small Babe" by Althouse, "Lullay My Liking," arranged*

10   *by Gustav Holst, "Tomorrow Shall Be My Dancing Day" by*

11   *Gardner, "Mary's Little Boy Child," arranged by Hairston, and*

12   *the Polish carol "Gloria, Gloria," arranged by Caldwell.])*

13   *SONG:*   "Lullay My Liking."

14   **SINGERS:**   *(Singing)* **Lullay my liking, my dear love, my**

15   **sweeting;**

16   **Lullay my dear heart, mine own dear darling.**

17   **I saw a fair maiden sitten and sing;**

18   **She lulled a little child, a sweet Lordling.**

19   **That Eternal Lord is he that made all things;**

20   **Of all Lordes, he is Lord, of every king he's King.**

21   **There was a mickle melody at that child's birth,**

22   **Though the songsters were heavenly**

23   **They made mickle mirth.**

24

25   **Angels bright they sang that night,**

26   **And saiden to that child,**

27   **"Blessed by Thou and so be she**

28   **That is so meek and mild.**

29   **Pray we now to that child, as to his mother dear,**

30   **God grant them all his blessing, that now maken cheer.**

31   *(Suggested song: "Tomorrow Shall Be My Dancing Day.")*

32   *(The DIRECTOR comes on. Looks at the audience for a long*

33   *moment, then goes to CHOIR DIRECTOR and whispers in his*

34   *or her ear. The CHOIR DIRECTOR nods. The DIRECTOR*

35   *comes down to the audience.)*

1   **DIRECTOR:**   I want to thank you for being so patient while
2   we rehearsed in front of you. We ... ah, we — well, *I* get
3   the feeling we'd all like to sing some carols here. *I'd* like
4   to sing some carols here. I think you probably know most
5   of these. Would you please sing along? Can we have more
6   light in here? *(House lights come up a bit. The CHOIR*
7   *DIRECTOR directs the audience to stand and leads them in the*
8   *Christmas carol sing-along section. [The original production*
9   *used carols about the angels: "The First Noel," "Angels We Have*
10   *Heard on High," "Hark! the Herald Angels Sing!"] At the close*
11   *of the carol sing-along, SHOPPERS ONE, TWO and THREE,*
12   *loaded down with presents, come to the front of the stage.)*
13   **SHOPPER ONE:**   One gift. That's all I really wanted to find.
14   **SHOPPER TWO:**   One gift.
15   **SHOPPER THREE:**   The perfect gift.
16   **SHOPPER ONE:**   Not just a tie ... or a CD ... or perfume.
17   **SHOPPER TWO:**   You know what kind of gift I'm talking
18   about, don't you? One that would just ... *make* a person's
19   whole Christmas season.
20   **SHOPPER THREE:**   His whole year.
21   **SHOPPER ONE:**   Maybe something that would ... I don't
22   know ... really change her life.
23   **SHOPPER TWO:**   Am I the only one who feels like that?
24   **SHOPPER THREE:**   Just once, I'd like to see someone I loved
25   get a gift that would really make a difference in his life.
26   **SHOPPER ONE:**   One she'd always cherish.
27   **SHOPPER TWO:**   One he could look back on and know
28   something changed that day.
29   **SHOPPER THREE:**   A gift that, once she had it, she'd wonder
30   how she ever lived without it.
31   **SHOPPER ONE:**   Yeah, that's the kind of gift I'd like to give
32   this year.
33   **SHOPPER TWO:**   That's the kind of gift I'd like to *get* this
34   year. *(The SHOPPERS freeze. The music begins for the next*
35   *song. The SHOPPERS return to their seats in the audience. The*

1	*SINGERS perform the carol. Suggested song: "The Star Carol."*
2	*At the close of the carol, the DIRECTOR comes up. He or she*
3	*starts talking to the SINGERS, but then turns to include the*
4	*audience.)*
5	**DIRECTOR: Thank you, choir. Can I ask you to do**
6	**something? While you're running around this week —**
7	**look for Jesus. He might be a little hard to spot in the**
8	**mall, between the gift wrap and the perfume department.**
9	**But you can find him. And if you're having trouble**
10	**figuring out where he is, maybe you can ask him to look**
11	**for you. I'm sure you're on his Christmas list. Good night.**
12	*(The DIRECTOR starts to go, but stops. He or she winks at the*
13	*SINGERS, then turns to the audience.)* **Oh, by the way . . .**
14	*(The DIRECTOR smiles and pulls out a long, crumpled*
15	*Christmas list and holds it up. And so do all the SINGERS.)*
16	**EVERYONE: Merry Christmas!** *(The lights come up, bright. So*
17	*do the house lights. The SINGERS break into "We Wish You a*
18	*Merry Christmas." They sing as they go up and out the aisles.)*
19	*SONG:* "We Wish You a Merry Christmas."
20	**SINGERS:** *(Singing)* **We wish you a merry Christmas,**
21	**We wish you a merry Christmas,**
22	**We wish you a merry Christmas,**
23	**And a happy New Year!**
24	
25	**Good tidings we bring**
26	**To you and your kin:**
27	**We wish you a Merry Christmas**
28	**And a happy New Year.**
29	
30	**Now bring us some figgy pudding,**
31	**Now bring us some figgy pudding,**
32	**Now bring us some figgy pudding,**
33	**And bring some out here.**
34	
35	**For we all like figgy pudding,**

1	For we all like figgy pudding,
2	For we all like figgy pudding,
3	So bring some out here.
4	
5	And we won't go until we get some,
6	We won't go until we get some,
7	We won't go until we get some,
8	So bring some out here!
9	
10	Good tidings we bring
11	To you and your kin,
12	Good tidings of Christmas,
13	And a happy New Year.
14	
15	We wish you a merry Christmas,
16	We wish you a merry Christmas,
17	We wish you a merry Christmas,
18	And a happy New Year.
19	
20	
21	
22	
23	
24	
25	
26	
27	
28	
29	
30	
31	
32	
33	
34	
35	

THE KING WHO HATED CHRISTMAS

A Christmas
Musical
Fairy Tale

L. G. Enscoe
Annie Enscoe

Lisa Rowland and Larry Enscoe in the Glendale Presbyterian Church
production of *The King Who Hated Christmas*

THE KING WHO HATED CHRISTMAS

CAST

SAMMY
(Surfer dude)

DAVIS
(Art student type)

GWEN
(Rich girl)

KING CORNELIUS

LUMP

THE VILLAGERS OF JEWELSHIRE
(A multigenerational choir)

VILLAGE MATRIARCH

HARD-OF-HEARING VILLAGER

VILLAGER ONE

VILLAGER TWO

VILLAGER THREE

VILLAGER FOUR

VILLAGE MAN ONE

VILLAGE MAN TWO

VILLAGE KID ONE

VILLAGE KID TWO

VILLAGE KID THREE
(And additional nonspeaking Village Kids if desired)

YOUNG VILLAGE WOMAN

CAST
(continued)

VILLAGE CHILD ONE

VILLAGE CHILD TWO

LITTLE GIRL

MRS. O'CEDAR

SERVANT ONE

SERVANT TWO

MUSIC MEISTER
(Choir Director)

CHILDREN'S CHOIR

ORCHESTRA
(If available)

PRODUCTION NOTES

Running Time

Seventy-five minutes.

Props

Battered trunk; book; skateboards; jingle bells; crown; scepter; decorations (greenery, bows, ribbons, etc.); candles; broom; hay cart; lamppost; signpost; benches; tree stumps; artificial snow; scrolls made of parchment paper; Western Union hat; bran muffin; birthday candle; party blower; kazoo or horn; visor; calculator; quill pen; sheets of music; beefeater hat; earmuffs; manger figures: Mary, Joseph, baby Jesus with manger; straw; Christmas lights (unlit when program starts).

Optional: Brightly colored banners with symbols of Jesus the King.

Costumes

All the Villagers and Actors wear medieval costumes. They may want to choose a costume according to a town position: a parson, the mayor, a constable, a tradesperson, etc. You can make your own, (see costume notes for *Call for the Lights and Sing!*) or you can rent them, which is how we always solved the problem. You can find patterns at fabric stores, and you can buy costume books in drama bookstores that will give you an idea of how things looked.

Since this program is performed in a "Fractured Fairy Tale" style, we tricked out each medieval costume with something contemporary: tennis shoes, a baseball cap, a Walkman, knee pads, a tux jacket, a fanny pack, etc.

The King should be dressed in an outrageous, mismatched costume. We used bright orange tights, tennis shoes sprayed and glittered with gold, a purple doublet, a bright red cape, and a huge gaudy crown.

Lump was dressed like a comic page boy.

The Musicians, including the Music Meister, were dressed as medieval troubadors. These included short capes and Three

81

Musketeers-like hats with feathers.

The medieval in medieval costumes is, of course, a very loose interpretation.

Set

The set is a medieval village square, but really only a few things On-stage suggest this: a hay cart, wooden benches, barrels, a signpost, and perhaps some fake snow on the ground (which you can find at any hobby, floral supply or arts and crafts store — especially around Christmas).

The risers may be covered with a tarp painted to look like stone steps. We also created a forest of Christmas trees, to the right and left, just off the platform. We flocked these and strung them with lights.

SUGGESTED MUSIC SOURCES

The following is music that was used in the original production:

"Gloria in Excelsis Deo," arr. Bob Krogstad, Integrity Music.

"A Festive Christmas Medley," Leslie Briccuse and Victor Young, from the Christmas musical "Glory," arr. Bob Krogstad, Singspiration, a division of the Benson Music Group.

"The Virgin Mary Had a Baby Boy," arr. by Camp Kirkland and Tom Fettke, Lillenas Publishing Co.

"The King of Glory Comes," Willard F. Jabusch, the Hymnal of the United Church of Christ.

"How Should a King Come," Jimmy and Carol Owens, Royal Tapestry (a division of Spectra, Inc.).

"The Way He Came," Mark Harris, Benson Music Group.

Thou Didst Leave Thy Throne," Emily E. S. Elliott and Timothy R. Matthews. (This can be found in any hymnal.)

"Thou Who Wast Rich," Frank Houghton, arr. John R. Dennis, J. R. Dennis Music.

"Christmas Hymn," Amy Grant and Michael W. Smith.

"O Happy Day Medley," arr. Mark Hayes, Word Music.

"Canticle of Joy," Camp Kirkland and Tom Fettke, Lillenas Publishing Co.

"Lift High the Lord, Our Banner," Macon Deavan, arr. Bob Krogstad, Integrity Music.

"All Hail, King Jesus," Dave Moody, arr. Gary Rhodes; Alleluia Music, Word Music.

"Glory," from the Christmas musical "Glory," arr. Bob Krogstad, Singspiration, a division of the Benson Music Group.

AUTHORS' NOTES

A "Fractured Fairy Tale." Remember those? Those slyly humorous cartoons that came on during the "Rocky and Bullwinkle Show."

Well, that's the model for "The King Who Hated Christmas." It's a tongue-in-cheek "fairy tale" about a king who discovers the King of kings. It's meant to be performed in a very theatrical style, taking time to wring every bad joke and pun.

But it's also very much not a fairy tale. It's also very much a conversion story. The humor only serves to set the important moments in relief, making them all the more powerful and moving.

In the original production, we opened with the kids on the sanctuary floor, then moved them to a higher platform to allow them to watch and comment on the action below.

The orchestra was very helpful in providing sound effects — trills, crashes, a well-placed glissando. Have fun scoring the program with clever, cartoon-like noises — either live or taped.

The program ends on a very worshipful note. Having worked through the images of earthly kings, then the heavenly King, the evening ends with a time of worship by his servants.

1   *(The congregation comes into the sanctuary or hall to soft carols*
2   *playing [taped or live]. On the platform, all that is lit are a few*
3   *fallen tree trunks making a semicircle around a battered old*
4   *trunk. Everything is covered in a dusting of snow. The overture*
5   *begins. The lights in the sanctuary or hall fade. We listen to the*
6   *music in near-darkness.*
7   *(During the music and darkness, the CHOIR comes in and gets*
8   *into place on the platform and in the aisles. They freeze in little*
9   *vignettes — greeting each other, doing chores, exchanging*
10 *presents, talking and laughing. [From now on the CHOIR will*
11 *be called VILLAGERS. They are multigenerational — adults,*
12 *teenagers, and children.]*
13 *(At the end of the overture, a strange noise is heard. It sounds*
14 *like . . . skateboards. Teenagers, SAMMY, DAVIS and GWEN,*
15 *on skateboards come down the aisles. They are dressed like*
16 *contemporary boarders, but each has a medieval touch, such as*
17 *a hat, a tunic, or knee boots. GWEN also has a wreath of flowers*
18 *around her head and carries a bunch of jingle bells. They skate*
19 *to the playing area, yelling encouragements to each other across*
20 *the sanctuary. Then:)*
21 **DAVIS: Friends, what think you will be our Christmas gifts**
22 **on the morrow?**
23 **SAMMY: I hath requested two turtledoves this year. But I'll**
24 **probably just get a geeky old partridge in a pear tree.**
25 **GWEN: My father hath promised me . . .** *(Sings)* **. . .** *fiiive*
26 *gooolden riiings!*
27 **DAVIS: Yeah, two for this ear. Two for that ear. And a big one**
28 **for thy nose!**
29 **SAMMY:** *(Approving)* **Dude-th!** *(SAMMY and DAVIS laugh and*
30 *high-five.)*
31 **GWEN:** *(Stomping away)* **Ah, hie you both hence! Dweebs!** *(She*
32 *bumps into the trunk.)* **Ho! What strange box is this?** *(She*
33 *starts fiddling with it.)*
34 **DAVIS:** *(Spooky)* **Perhaps 'tis a coffin! Filled with bones of an**
35 **evil ogre!**

1   **GWEN:** *(Jumping back, freaked)* **Get out of my face-eth.**

2   **SAMMY:** *(Simply)* **Perhaps 'tis a treasure chest.** *(They look at*

3   *each other. They all dive at the trunk, trying to break into it. It*

4   *snaps open. They lift the lid. A magical trill. A light change.*

5   *The VILLAGERS move a bit [still silent], then freeze again. The*

6   *world of the story is starting to come to life. Meanwhile, SAMMY,*

7   *DAVIS and GWEN are frantically digging inside the trunk.*

8   *Nothing.)*

9   **DAVIS:** **Empty as a pocket!**

10   **SAMMY:** *Booogus!*

11   **GWEN:** **Not so quick, my friends! There's something hidden**

12   **inside!** *(She pulls out a huge, ancient book.)* **Look, Sammy!**

13   **Look, Davis! 'Tis a book!**

14   **SAMMY and DAVIS:** *(Totally unexcited)* **Whoa . . . excellent.**

15   *(She blows the dust off the book. A magical trill. Light change.*

16   *The VILLAGERS move again — then freeze. SAMMY, DAVIS*

17   *or GWEN don't see the people all around them.)*

18   **GWEN:** *(Sits on the trunk and reads the cover.)* **"The King Who**

19   **Hated Christmas." Or, "How King Cornelius Stopped**

20   **Being a Royal Pain and Figured Out You Can't Play**

21   **Quartet in the Trinity."**

22   **SAMMY and DAVIS:** *(False excitement)* **Sounds great-eth!** *(They*

23   *look at each other.)* **Not!** *(They grab their boards and split. GWEN*

24   *opens the book. A magical trill. Light change. The VILLAGERS*

25   *move — and freeze. At the trill, SAMMY and DAVIS stop and*

26   *look up. Did they hear something? They shrug and move off*

27   *down an aisle.)*

28   **GWEN:** *(Reading out loud)* **"Once upon a time there was a king**

29   **who loathed Christmas with such a loathsome loath, that**

30   **one year he huffed, and he puffed, and called the whole**

31   **thing off!"** *(SAMMY and DAVIS halt in their tracks. They turn*

32   *and look at her. They're hooked.)*

33   **SAMMY:** **It say-eth not that!**

34   **GWEN:** *(Knows she's got them.)* **Yeah-huh.** *(Reads.)* **"It all**

35   **happened in the happy, healthy, high-spirited little**

1   **hamlet known as Jewelshire."** *(Or make up a town based on*
2   *your city. Another trill. The VILLAGERS move — and freeze. A*
3   *light comes up on a rugged, cartoon-like signpost just off the*
4   *platform. The arrows point off in different directions —*
5   *"Jewelshire," "King's Castle," "Dark Forest," "Magic Kingdom,"*
6   *and "Bakersfield" [Or cities based on your area]. GWEN teases*
7   *them.)* **Oh . . . you lads care not for this story.** *(She smiles*
8   *and slams the book closed. The light snaps off the signpost.)*
9 **SAMMY and DAVIS:** *Yeah-huh! (They act cool. Turning to each*
10   *other)*
11 **DAVIS:** **Hast thou anything to do on this Christmas Eve,**
12   **Sammy?**
13 **SAMMY:** **Not I, Davis.**
14 **DAVIS:** **I thought not.**
15 **SAMMY and DAVIS:** *(To GWEN)* **Read-eth!** *(GWEN shrugs. She*
16   *opens the book. Another trill. Light up on the signpost. The*
17   *VILLAGERS move — and freeze.)*
18 **GWEN:** *(Reading)* **"Oh, King Cornelius was an angry king.**
19   **The villagers of Jewelshire hung heavy under the burden**
20   **of his ire, his taxes, and his really bad taste in clothes."**
21   *(We hear an awful chord. A spotlight picks up KING*
22   *CORNELIUS. He looks like a Royal Doof dressed in a traditional*
23   *fairy-tale king costume with nothing matching. Horrible colors.*
24   *He wears gold high-top tennis shoes. Carries a goofy scepter.*
25   *Wears a giant, gaudy, jewel-encrusted crown. He walks to his*
26   *"kingdom" with a haughty sneer. Behind his back, LUMP,*
27   *dressed as the king's jester, mimics his walk and expression. The*
28   *KIDS don't notice him. GWEN reads.)*
29   **"King Cornelius was especially nasty as he walked**
30   **his kingdom every Christmas Eve. He** *hated* **the laughter.**
31   **He** *hated* **the festivity. But most of all, he** *hated* **that Jesus**
32   **got more adoration than he did."**
33 **KING CORNELIUS:** *(To the audience)* **And he gets all the great**
34   **presents, too!**
35 **GWEN:** **"No one knew why the king began hating Christmas.**

1   But I think the likeliest reason of all may have been that
2   his heart was two sizes too small —"
3 KING CORNELIUS: *(To the KIDS) **That was the Grinch, you***
4   ***little toads!***
5 LUMP: ***Toads!*** *(SAMMY, DAVIS and GWEN suddenly look up,*
6   *terrified. They see KING CORNELIUS walking toward them!*
7   *The guys look at GWEN, as if the KING was her fault.)*
8 SAMMY: **What did you do-eth?!**
9 GWEN: **I was just using my imagination!**
10 DAVIS: **Run away-eth!**
11 SAMMY: **Run away-eth!** ***Run away-eth!*** *(They take off. GWEN*
12   *doubles back, dropping her jingle bells, and grabs the book —*
13   *barely escaping the KING.)*
14 KING CORNELIUS: **That's right! Run away-eth!**
15 LUMP: **Run away-eth!**
16 KING CORNELIUS: **If you're so afraid of your imagination,**
17   **run home and watch TV!** *(He looks down and sees the jingle*
18   *bells GWEN has dropped. He picks them up and jingles them.*
19   *An evil sneer)* **Ha! Another yuletide eve has come. But this**
20   **year I'll see no "merry Christmases" done!** *(A sudden bright*
21   *fanfare comes from the back of the sanctuary. KING*
22   *CORNELIUS hisses and hies off the platform. LUMP does the*
23   *same thing and follows him. We hear GWEN's voice, reading*
24   *from the book.)*
25 GWEN: *(Recorded or Off-stage)* **"Yet in spite of creepy, cranky,**
26   **cantankerous King Cornelius, Christmas came to**
27   **Jewelshire all the same."**
28   *(The lights come up. The VILLAGERS suddenly come to life.*
29   *They start singing a festive opening number as they head for the*
30   *platform — something like "Joy to the World." [The original*
31   *production used "Gloria in Excelsis Deo" by Krogstad.] This*
32   *should be a joyous song about Christ's birth. The VILLAGERS*
33   *vibrantly greet each other, greet the congregation, and exchange*
34   *gifts as they sing and move toward the platform.)*
35 *SONG:* "Joy to the World."

1   **VILLAGERS:** *(Singing)* **Joy to the world! the Lord is come;**
2   **Let earth receive her King;**
3   **Let every heart prepare him room,**
4   **And heaven and nature sing,**
5   **And heaven and nature sing,**
6   **And heaven, and heaven and nature sing.**
7
8   **Joy to the world! the Savior reigns:**
9   **Let men their songs employ;**
10   **While fields and floods, rocks, hills and plains,**
11   **Repeat the sounding joy,**
12   **Repeat the sounding joy,**
13   **Repeat, repeat the sounding joy.**
14
15   **No more let sins and sorrows grow,**
16   **Nor thorns infest the ground;**
17   **He comes to make his blessings flow**
18   **Far as the curse is found,**
19   **Far as the curse is found,**
20   **Far as, far as the curse is found.**
21
22   **He rules the world with truth and grace,**
23   **And makes the nations prove**
24   **The glories of his righteousness,**
25   **And wonders of his love,**
26   **And wonders of his love,**
27   **And wonders, wonders of his love.**
28 **VILLAGER ONE:**   **Tomorrow day is Christmas morn!**
29 **VILLAGER TWO:**   **When this tired, old world became reborn!**
30 **VILLAGER THREE:** **Bring out the color, so the day can be**
31   **met!**
32 **VILLAGER FOUR:** **Bring out the props so the stage can be**
33   **set!**
34   *(The VILLAGERS launch into another festive song, or perhaps*
35   *a pastiche of songs celebrating the season or a song that allows*

1   *some acting out of holiday moments. [The original production*
2   *used "A Festive Christmas Medley" by Bricusse/Young. Feel free*
3   *to place your own choices here.] As the VILLAGERS sing, props*
4   *are brought up onto the playing area: a car, lamppost, house*
5   *front, benches, etc. All the elements to create a village square.*
6   *(Some of the VILLAGERS take the props and place them. One*
7   *VILLAGER (MRS. O'CEDAR) sweeps the stage with a rickety*
8   *broom. Another VILLAGER comes behind her, throwing*
9   *snowflakes on the ground. Other VILLAGERS bring in garland,*
10   *bows, ribbons and pine boughs and decorate the square. At the*
11   *close of the song, there's a magical trill and the VILLAGERS*
12   *freeze.*
13   *(A spotlight picks up SAMMY, DAVIS and GWEN sitting on a*
14   *side platform [or, perhaps, above the action]. GWEN is staring*
15   *in terror at a page in the book.)*
16   **SAMMY: Why hath you stopped your reading?**
17   **GWEN: The king 'tis about to return to the village!**
18   **DAVIS: Aw, be not a wimp!**
19   **SAMMY and DAVIS: Read-eth!** *(From the back of the sanctuary*
20   *screeches the worst trumpet fanfare anyone has ever heard. The*
21   *VILLAGERS unfreeze and look at each other in horror.)*
22   **GWEN:**   *(Reading)* **" 'Twas a frightening sound that the jumpy**
23   **Jewelshirians could hear for miles . . .** *(She looks at*
24   *DAVIS.)* **. . . Davis."** *(The VILLAGERS groan in disgust and*
25   *look over at GWEN. She shrugs and keeps reading.)*
26   **" 'Twas   at   that   moment   contemptible   King**
27   **Cornelius began his Christmas Eve tour of his kingdom.**
28   **The sound of merriment and worship had been pounding**
29   **on his royal eardrums all day! And he was most**
30   **fearsomely furious! Now, please don't ask why. Nobody**
31   **knows the reason. Perhaps his head wasn't screwed**
32   **on just right. It could be perhaps that his shoes were**
33   **too —"**
34   **KING CORNELIUS:**   *(From the back)* **That was the Grinch, you**
35   **blithering goose!** *(KING CORNELIUS floats down the aisle,*

1 *carried on the shoulders of two SERVANTS dressed in jester*
2 *clothes. LUMP parades behind him, now with a bright bag slung*
3 *over his shoulder and carrying a horn. The VILLAGERS back*
4 *away, shuddering in terror. To the SERVANTS)* **Hurry up!**
5 **Faster! Put me down! Put me down!** *I said, put me down!*
6 SERVANT ONE: **OK, sire ... You're ugly and you have**
7 **absolutely no fashion sense.**
8 KING CORNELIUS: *Aggghhh! (The SERVANTS nearly drop*
9 *KING CORNELIUS as they set him down. He snarls at them*
10 *and they scurry out of the sanctuary. Then he turns to the*
11 *cowering VILLAGERS.)* **Greetings, village people! Your**
12 **sovereign, all-powerful king has a holiday message for**
13 **you this fair Christmas Eve.** *(In their faces)* **You've sung**
14 **your last "Noel," my little pretties! Hark! Give ear to the**
15 **proclamation. Lump ... ?** *(He sees LUMP is busy menacing*
16 *the VILLAGERS.)* **... Oh, Lump ... ?** *Luuump!*
17 LUMP: *(Snapping to)* **Sire, yes, sire!**
18 KING CORNELIUS: **Proclaim the proclamation!** *(LUMP*
19 *jumps up on a bench. He pulls a parchment scroll out of his sack*
20 *with great ceremony. It unfurls to the floor. He digs a Western*
21 *Union hat out and puts it on. He clears his throat.)*
22 LUMP: *(Reads in a cracking voice.)* **"By order of Cornelius,**
23 **King of Everything From Here to There and Back Again,**
24 **Christmas will no longer be held in celebration of the**
25 **birth of Christ! From this day forward and hence,**
26 **Christmas shall be called King Corny's Day. And you will**
27 **worship and celebrate the birth of** *our* **king!"**
28 HARD-OF-HEARING VILLAGER: **He say King Jesus ... ?**
29 KING CORNELIUS: **King Cornelius, you deaf old croak!**
30 *(Strokes his crown.)* **Can you all see this lovely crown? This**
31 **means** *I'm the king!* *(He turns to the audience.)* **Every year**
32 **Jesus gets worship ... and adoration ... and everybody**
33 **gets great presents. Do you know what I get on my**
34 **birthday? Show 'em, Lump!** *(LUMP pulls out a bran muffin,*
35 *sticks a candle in it, lights it and blows a party blower. He starts*

91

1   *playing "Happy Birthday" on a kazoo. It's awful.)* **Lump . . . oh,**
2   **Lumpy . . . *Luuump!*** *(LUMP stops. KING CORNELIUS points*
3   *at the quaking VILLAGERS. The SERVANTS appear carrying*
4   *the battered trunk. They set it down and scurry off.)*
5   **I want all of you to put those disgustingly cute**
6   **Christmas decorations in that trunk. Boughs! Bells!**
7   **Buttons! Bows!** *All of it! (LUMP holds the trunk open. The*
8   *VILLAGERS start stuffing all the decorations inside.)*
9   **Now, I want to hear** *no* **carols,** *no* **"merry**
10   **Christmases," and** *no* **presents — except those given to**
11   *me* **— and** *no* **mention of the name King Jesus!** *(The trunk*
12   *lid slams closed with a resounding boom.)*
13   **Tell me, Shiny Happy People! What is all this**
14   **worshiping of a king you've never even seen, hmmm?**
15   **What kind of king is this Jesus, anyway? Does he have a**
16   **crown? Does he even have a crown?!** *Lump, count the*
17   *royal jewels!*
18   **LUMP:**   **Excuse me, sire?**
19   **KING CORNELIUS:**   **The crown jewels, you dolt! I can't count**
20   **the jewels because my royal crown is on my royal head!**
21   **And I take my crown off for no man! Not even me. How**
22   **many?** *(LUMP puts on a visor, pulls out a calculator and starts*
23   *punching the buttons with a quill pen.)*
24   **LUMP:**   **Twenty-seven-and-a-half royal jewels, sire!**
25   **KING CORNELIUS:**   **There you are then! Dear Lump, give**
26   **them the music!** *(LUMP passes sheets of music around to the*
27   *VILLAGERS.)* **You will** *all* **learn this music for my**
28   **birthday tomorrow! It's the only carol I want to**
29   **hear . . . or else. Lump!**
30   **LUMP:**   **Yes, Your Awfulness?**
31   **KING CORNELIUS:**   **Remain here and see that no one breaks**
32   **the law!** *(Leans in close.)* **Watch them like a hawk . . . or I**
33   **will personally make sure you live up to your name . . .**
34   **LUMP:**   *(Gulping and shaking)* **Yes, Your Tackiness.**
35   **KING CORNELIUS:**   *Music Meister! (The CHOIR DIRECTOR*

1   *jumps up.)*

2 **CHOIR DIRECTOR:**   Sire!

3 **KING CORNELIUS:**   Conduct! *(The SERVANTS carry KING*

4   *CORNELIUS out on their shoulders. The CHOIR DIRECTOR*

5   *conducts the VILLAGERS in "Cornelius Birthday Carol," which*

6   *is a horrible birthday song extolling KING CORNELIUS, set to*

7   *the tune of the "Hallelujah Chorus." It consists of: Happy*

8   *birthday, happy birthday, King Cornelius, King Cornelius, King*

9   *Corneliiiuuusss" over and over. As KING CORNELIUS goes*

10   *out)* **Wonderful! Lovely! Adorable! Goosebumply!** *And alll*

11   *fooor mee! (A magic trill. The VILLAGERS freeze. Lights come*

12   *up on GWEN, SAMMY and DAVIS.)*

13 **SAMMY:**   Whoa, intense-eth.

14 **DAVIS:**   Indeed. Truly a bogus dude.

15 **GWEN:**   *(Reading)* **"All that Christmas Eve day, Lump stood**

16   **watch over the sad-hearted citizens of Jewelshire to**

17   **make certain no shred of Christmas was left intact."**

18   *(LUMP puts on a beefeater hat and starts goosestepping across*

19   *the stage chanting, "Doh-ee-oh, Doh-oh." The VILLAGERS*

20   *unfreeze and watch three vignettes:*

21   *(MRS. O'CEDAR starts sweeping, sadly. As she sweeps, she*

22   *starts to whistle a carol. LUMP spins and points at her. The*

23   *VILLAGERS gasp. MRS. O'CEDAR quickly starts whistling*

24   *another tune — such as the theme from "The Andy Griffith*

25   *Show." The VILLAGERS sigh in relief. LUMP goes back to*

26   *marching. Two VILLAGE MEN cross the stage.)*

27 **VILLAGE MAN ONE:**   Greetings, Sven!

28 **VILLAGE MAN TWO:**   Hi ya, Myron!

29 **VILLAGE MAN ONE:**   *Meeerrry . . . (LUMP points at the men.*

30   *The VILLAGERS gasp.)* **. . . had a little lamb!** *(The*

31   *VILLAGERS sigh in relief.)*

32 **VILLAGE MAN TWO:**   **The same to you and yours!** *(The*

33   *VILLAGE MEN walk off. LUMP goes on marching. Two*

34   *VILLAGE KIDS sneak toward each other with brightly wrapped*

35   *presents. They look around and quickly hand each other the*

1   *gifts. LUMP points at them, aghast. The VILLAGERS gasp!*
2   *The VILLAGE KIDS think fast:)*
3   **VILLAGE KID ONE:**   **Dude, thanks for lettin' me borrow your**
4   **festively wrapped *empty* box!**
5   **VILLAGE KID TWO:**   **Likewise, mon frere.** *(The VILLAGE KIDS*
6   *walk off. The VILLAGERS freeze. LUMP freezes mid-step.)*
7   **GWEN:**   *(Reading)* **An empty, black night swallowed joyless**
8   **Jewelshire. . ."** *(The lights go to night colors. The sound of*
9   *crickets is heard. A few lamps are lit. GWEN continues reading.)*
10   **". . . and Lump, tired of his long watch, fell into a *deeep***
11   ***sleeep.*"** *(LUMP suddenly falls down, dead asleep.)* **"And the**
12   **villagers decided they could hold back their Christmas**
13   **joy and celebration no longer!"**
14   *(The VILLAGERS unfreeze. A YOUNG VILLAGE WOMAN*
15   *shushes them and trots to LUMP, snoring on the ground. She*
16   *puts earmuffs on him, grins and runs back to the group. The*
17   *VILLAGERS begin to sing "The Virgin Mary Had a Baby Boy."*
18   *[Or another song about the child Jesus coming down from*
19   *heaven.] They enjoy the celebration — the secret spirit of*
20   *Christmas.)*
21   *SONG:*   "The Virgin Mary Had a Baby Boy."
22   **VILLAGERS:**   *(Singing)* **The Virgin Mary had a baby boy,**
23   **The Virgin Mary had a baby boy,**
24   **The Virgin Mary had a baby boy,**
25   **And they said that his name was Jesus.**
26
27   **And unto us a blessed child is born,**
28   **And unto us a blessed child is born,**
29   **And unto us a blessed child is born,**
30   **And they said that his name was Jesus.**
31
32   **He come from the glory,**
33   **He come from the glorious kingdom,**
34   **He come from the glory,**
35   **He come from the glorious kingdom.**

1	And he will be the Savior of the world,
2	And he will be the Savior of the world,
3	And he will be the Savior of the world,
4	And they said that his name was Jesus.
5	
6	He come from the glory,
7	He come from the glorious kingdom,
8	He come from the glory,
9	He come from the glorious kingdom.
10	*(At the close of the song, a soloist sings "O Come, All Ye*
11	*Faithful.")*
12	**SONG:** "O Come, All Ye Faithful." *(Verses 1 and 3)*
13	SOLOIST: *(Singing)* O Come, all ye faithful,
14	Joyful and triumphant,
15	O come ye, O come ye, to Bethlehem.
16	Come and behold him,
17	Born the King of angels;
18	
19	O come, let us adore him,
20	O come, let us adore him,
21	O come, let us adore him,
22	Christ the Lord.
23	
24	Yea, Lord, we greet thee,
25	Born this happy morning;
26	Jesus, to thee be all glory giv'n;
27	Word of the Father,
28	Now in flesh appearing;
29	
30	O come, let us adore him,
31	O come, let us adore him,
32	O come, let us adore him,
33	Christ the Lord.
34	GWEN: *(Reading)* "Then one of the sweet village children
35	stepped forward to ask this question."

1   **VILLAGE KID ONE:**   *(Jumping up on a stump)* **Hey! I'm a little**
2   **fuzzy on this king thing. If Jesus is a king, how come he**
3   **doesn't have a crown?**
4   **VILLAGE KID TWO:**   **How come he doesn't live in a castle?**
5   **VILLAGE KID THREE:**   **How come he doesn't arrive with his**
6   **royal armies and bring Christmas back to Jewelshire?!**
7   *(A cheer goes up from the VILLAGE KIDS. Here the villagers*
8   *sing a song about what kind of King Jesus Christ really is.*
9   *Suggested song: "The King of Glory Comes." [The original*
10   *production used "How Should a King Come?"]*
11   *(A trio follows this song with another about Jesus the King and*
12   *what he gave up to take on human form. Perhaps something like*
13   *"Thou Didst Leave Thy Throne." [The original production used*
14   *"The Way He Came" by Harris.])*
15   *SONG:*   "Thou Didst Leave Thy Throne."
16   **TRIO:**   *(Singing)* **Thou didst leave thy throne and thy kingly**
17   **crown,**
18   **When thou camest to earth for me,**
19   **But in Bethlehem's home there was found no room,**
20   **For thy holy nativity.**
21   *CHORUS:*   **O come to my heart, Lord Jesus:**
22   **There is room in my heart for thee!**
23
24   **Heaven's arches rang when the angels sang,**
25   **Proclaiming thy royal degree,**
26   **But in lowly birth didst thou come to earth**
27   **And in great humility.**
28   *CHORUS*
29   **The foxes found rest, and the birds their nest**
30   **In the shade of the forest tree,**
31   **But thy couch was the sod, O thou Son of God,**
32   **In the deserts of Galilee.**
33   *CHORUS*
34   **Thou camest, O Lord, with the living Word**
35   **That should set thy people free,**

1   But with mocking scorn and with crown of thorn

2   They bore thee to Calvary.

3   **CHORUS**

4   When the heavens shall ring and the angels sing

5   At thy coming to victory,

6   Let thy voice call me home, saying,

7   "Yet there is room, there is room at my side for thee."

8   **CHORUS**

9   *(The VILLAGE MATRIARCH comes forward and sits. A group*

10   *of VILLAGE KIDS sits at her feet.)*

11   **VILLAGE MATRIARCH:**   It's not having wealth that brings

12   happiness and joy at Christmas time. It's knowing

13   someone believes *you* are a treasure. King Jesus became

14   the greatest King by giving everything he had — even his

15   life — to *you*, the greatest gift of all. A *real* king loves his

16   people *that* much. You are the jewels in his crown! *(The*

17   *VILLAGE MATRIARCH, still seated with the kids around her,*

18   *sings a solo. Suggested song: "Thou Who Wast Rich."*

19   *(LUMP suddenly awakes. He jumps to his feet, giving all the*

20   *VILLAGERS a glare. He smacks his lips and continues his*

21   *guard. A light comes up on GWEN.)*

22   **GWEN:**   *(Reading)* "With sad hearts full of loud praise now

23   silent, the villagers of Jewelshire took to their beds." *(The*

24   *VILLAGERS slowly turn their backs to the audience. They blow*

25   *out the candles and lamps. They sit on the risers and sleep on*

26   *each other's shoulders, snoring loudly. The lights fade to black.*

27   *Then a spot comes up on GWEN, SAMMY and DAVIS.)*

28   **DAVIS:**   Is that the end of the story?

29   **SAMMY:**   They just missed Christmas?

30   **GWEN:**   Who's reading this tale?

31   **SAMMY and DAVIS:**   Thou art.

32   **GWEN:**   *(Reading)* "Late that Christmas Eve, King Cornelius

33   had a thought — a nasty, sneaky, creepy little thought."

34   *(A spotlight picks up KING CORNELIUS in the aisle.)*

35   **KING CORNELIUS:**   I think I'll just hide among the villagers

1   **and see just what they have planned for my birthday**
2   **tomorrow!** *Oooo,* **that's nasty. And sneaky.**
3   **GWEN, SAMMY and DAVIS: And creepy.**
4   **KING CORNELIUS: Shut up!** *(KING CORNELIUS vogues to the*
5   *playing area. The lights come up, revealing an empty square.)*
6   **GWEN:** *(Reading)* **"But when the king reached the village**
7   **square, he heard only the snoring of the people, lost in**
8   **the dreams of Christmases past."** *(The VILLAGERS snore.*
9   *KING CORNELIUS even finds LUMP sprawled on the steps*
10   *and snoring. GWEN continues reading.)* **"The king was about**
11   **to fly into a fearsomely fearful rage. But he heard a noise.**
12   **It was the sound of children. Children up way past their**
13   **bedtimes."** *(VILLAGE CHILDREN's voices are heard in the*
14   *darkness, shushing each other and saying, "This way" and "Over*
15   *here!" KING CORNELIUS jumps behind the trunk and watches.*
16   *Three VILLAGE CHILDREN sneak into the middle of the*
17   *square: Two OLDER CHILDREN and a LITTLE GIRL.)*
18   **VILLAGE CHILD ONE:** *(Whispering)* **Did you bring it?**
19   *(VILLAGE CHILD TWO nods, looks at VILLAGE CHILD*
20   *THREE.)*
21   **VILLAGE CHILD TWO: Did** *you* **bring it?** *(VILLAGE CHILD*
22   *THREE nods.)*
23   **VILLAGE CHILD ONE: Cool. Let's have a look.** *(They pull out*
24   *manger figures from their pockets.)* **I have Mary.**
25   **VILLAGE CHILD TWO: I have Joseph.**
26   **LITTLE GIRL: And I got the baby Jesus!** *(They arrange the manger*
27   *figures on a stump or a bench. The music for a children's Christmas*
28   *song begins — something like "Away in a Manger." [The original*
29   *production used "Christmas Hymn" by Amy Grant and Michael W.*
30   *Smith.] The CHILDREN'S CHOIR appears behind the VILLAGE*
31   *KIDS and the manger figures. During the song, the VILLAGE*
32   *CHILDREN may put a handful of straw around the figures.)*
33   *SONG:* "Away in a Manger."
34   **CHILDREN'S CHOIR:** *(Singing)* **Away in a manger, no crib for**
35   **a bed,**

1   The little Lord Jesus laid down his sweet head.
2   The stars in the sky
3   Looked down where he lay,
4   The little Lord Jesus, asleep on the hay.
5
6   The cattle are lowing, the baby awakes,
7   But little Lord Jesus, no crying he makes.
8   I love thee, Lord Jesus!
9   Look down from the sky,
10   And stay by my cradle till morning is nigh.
11
12   Be near me, Lord Jesus! I ask thee to stay
13   Close by me forever, and love me, I pray.
14   Bless all the dear children
15   In thy tender care,
16   And fit us for heaven to live with thee there.
17   *(KING CORNELIUS wipes away a tear at the end of the song.)*
18   **VILLAGE CHILD ONE:**   I hope you all know that we've put
19   ourselves in big-time danger by doing this.
20   **VILLAGE CHILD TWO:**   If King Cornelius finds out . . .
21   **LITTLE GIRL:**   Why does King Cornelius hate Jesus so much?
22   **VILLAGE CHILD ONE:**   He doesn't hate him, goofy. He just
23   doesn't know him.
24   **VILLAGE CHILD TWO:**   If he did, he'd give Jesus his crown
25   in a heartbeat.
26   **KING   CORNELIUS:** ***Whaaat?!*** *(The   VILLAGE   KIDS   and*
27   *CHILDREN'S CHOIR scream and run Off-stage. LUMP startles*
28   *awake and watches in terror. KING CORNELIUS stomps to the*
29   *manger scene. The LITTLE GIRL runs back On-stage to grab*
30   *the baby Jesus. KING CORNELIUS grabs her by the scruff of*
31   *her neck and snatches the figure out of her hand.)*
32   **LITTLE GIRL:**   Please, Your Great Big Majesty Highness
33   Sire! Lemme take the baby Jesus home. It's just not
34   Christmas   around   my   house   without   'im!   *(KING*
35   *CORNELIUS glares at her, then at the figure.)*

1   **KING CORNELIUS:**   Do . . . do you mind if I keep him here for
2   **a little while?** *(The LITTLE GIRL thinks about it a moment.)*
3   **LITTLE GIRL:**   **Well . . . OK, Your Majesty. But you hafta put**
4   **'im in the cradle like this. See?** *(She takes the baby Jesus*
5   *and puts him back in the cradle.)* **And before you open your**
6   **presents and stuff, you hafta pray and thank 'im for**
7   **everything — you know, because you got a lotta neat**
8   **stuff. Stuff you don't deserve, but he gives it to ya anyway.**
9   *(The LITTLE GIRL kneels down. She looks up at KING*
10   *CORNELIUS. She tugs on his cuff. KING CORNELIUS rolls*
11   *his eyes and kneels.)*
12   **KING CORNELIUS:**   **What . . . stuff?**
13   **LITTLE GIRL:**   **Like . . . well, like life. And not bein' sick. And**
14   **the mountains and stuff. And your castle. And that**
15   **radical crown. See, he's the King. He's even** *your* **King.**
16   **Well, Your Highness . . . farewell!** *(The LITTLE GIRL starts*
17   *to run Off-stage, but stops.)* **Sire?**
18   **KING CORNELIUS:**   **Yes?**
19   **LITTLE GIRL:**   **Merry Christmas!** *(She plants a kiss on his cheek*
20   *and takes off. KING CORNELIUS is touched. He doesn't know*
21   *what to say. He looks over at LUMP, who looks like he might*
22   *faint from shock.)*
23   **KING CORNELIUS:**   **Got something to say about that, knave?!**
24   **LUMP:**   **M . . . Mer . . . Mer —**
25   **KING CORNELIUS:**   **Spit it out!**
26   **LUMP:**   *Merry Christmas, sire!* *(KING CORNELIUS comes at*
27   *him. LUMP closes his eyes and waits for his doom. KING*
28   *CORNELIUS puts his arm around him.)*
29   **KING CORNELIUS:**   **The same to you, Lumpy.** *(A soloist comes*
30   *forward and sings "What Child Is This?", verses one and three.*
31   *The VILLAGERS join quietly in the background. KING*
32   *CORNELIUS is staring at the manger figures.)*
33   *SONG:*   "What Child Is This?"
34   **SOLOIST:**   *(Singing)* **What child is this, who, laid to rest**
35   **On Mary's lap is sleeping?**

1   **Whom angels greet with anthems sweet**
2   **While shepherds watch are keeping?**
3

4   **This, this is Christ the King,**
5   **Whom shepherds guard and angels sing;**
6   **Haste, haste to bring him laud,**
7   **The babe, the son of Mary!**
8

9   **So bring him incense, gold, and myrrh,**
10   **Come, peasant, king to own him;**
11   **The King of kings salvation brings,**
12   **Let loving hearts enthrone him.**
13   *(At this moment, KING CORNELIUS goes to the manger figures.*
14   *He kneels down, staring closely at them. He reaches up for his*
15   *crown.)*
16   **Raise, raise the song on high,**
17   **The virgin sing her lullaby;**
18   **Joy! Joy! for Christ is born,**
19   **The babe, the son of Mary!**
20   *(After the song is finished, the VILLAGERS turn so their backs*
21   *are to the audience. KING CORNELIUS takes his crown off.*
22   *LUMP stares in amazement. KING CORNELIUS hesitates, then*
23   *lays the crown at the manger. KING CORNELIUS turns and*
24   *strides off down the aisle. LUMP follows him out in wonder. The*
25   *lights go to blackout.)*
26   **GWEN:**   *(Reading)* **"The Christmas sun rose on a village of**
27   **long faces and heavy hearts. As usual, Mrs. O'Cedar was**
28   **up at dawn to sweep the front of her shop."** *(The lights*
29   *come up. It's morning. The VILLAGERS still have their backs*
30   *to the audience. MRS. O'CEDAR turns around and starts*
31   *sweeping. She sweeps to the bench with the manger figures. Her*
32   *mouth drops open. Her eyes go wide. She's looking at KING*
33   *CORNELIUS's crown lying at the feet of the baby Jesus.)*
34   **MRS. O'CEDAR:**   *(In shock)* **Crown!** *Crown!* *(She starts turning*
35   *the VILLAGERS around.)* **Crown! Crown!**

1   **VILLAGER ONE:**   **Crown? Was Jack up on that hill again?**

2   **VILLAGER TWO:**   **With Jill?** *(MRS. O'CEDAR points to the crown*

3   *at the manger. The VILLAGERS awaken and turn to see the*

4   *crown. They all bubble in amazement.)*

5   **GWEN:**   *(Reading)* **"And with the strange, amazing sight of**

6   **King Cornelius's crown lying at the feet of the baby Jesus,**

7   **everybody knew that Christmas had come back to**

8   **Jewelshire!"**

9   **VILLAGER THREE:**   **Look! Christmas has come back to**

10   **Jewelshire!**

11   **MRS. O'CEDAR:**   **Everybody knows that.**

12   **VILLAGER THREE:**   **Oh.** *(The VILLAGERS break into "Go,*

13   *Tell It on the Mountain," or another praise song celebrating the*

14   *Christmas story. [The original production used the "O Happy*

15   *Day Medley," arranged by Hayes.])*

16   *SONG:*   "Go, Tell It on the Mountain."

17   **VILLAGERS:**   *(Singing)*

18   *REFRAIN:*   **Go, tell it on the mountain,**

19   **Over the hills and everywhere.**

20   **Go, tell it on the mountain**

21   **That Jesus Christ is born!**

22

23   **While shepherds kept their watching**

24   **O'er silent flocks by night,**

25   **Behold throughout the heavens**

26   **There shone a holy light.**

27   *REFRAIN*

28   **The shepherds feared and trembled**

29   **When lo! Above the earth**

30   **Rang out the angel chorus**

31   **That hailed our Savior's birth.**

32   *(KING CORNELIUS is suddenly there — sans crown. The*

33   *VILLAGERS are astounded. He sings with them on the refrain,*

34   *and then takes the next verse.)*

35   *REFRAIN*

1 KING CORNELIUS: *(Singing solo)* **Down in a lowly manger**
2   **The humble Christ was born,**
3   **And brought us God's salvation**
4   **That blessed Christmas morn.**
5 *REFRAIN*
6   *(The VILLAGERS cheer at the end of the song. KING*
7   *CORNELIUS goes into the crowd and begins shaking their*
8   *hands.)*
9 GWEN: *(Reading)* **"As they sang their song of celebration,**
10   **King Cornelius chose to show up without royal display.**
11   **And they say his heart grew three sizes that day."**
12 KING CORNELIUS and VILLAGERS: *(Turning on GWEN)*
13   ***That was the Grinch!***
14 KING CORNELIUS: **Friends! Christmas survives without**
15   **presents and bows!**
16   **It survives even without bells, baubles and snow.**
17   **But without the King, the day cannot be sound.**
18   **Especially when the King of kings is finally found!**
19   *(The VILLAGERS cheer and applaud. KING CORNELIUS*
20   *calls:)* **Lump!** ***Luuump!*** *(LUMP leads the two SERVANTS*
21   *carrying the trunk down the center aisle.)* **Lump, break open**
22   **the treasure inside the box! Let us see color in Jewelshire!**
23 GWEN: *(Reading)* **"And there was such joy to the world as**
24   **was never heard in any hamlet of any kingdom on earth!"**
25   *(As the VILLAGERS pull their Christmas decorations from the*
26   *trunk and hang them, they sing an upbeat carol. Suggested song:*
27   *"How Great Our Joy!" During this time, one of the VILLAGERS*
28   *places CORNELIUS's crown back inside the trunk. [The original*
29   *production used "Canticle of Joy," arranged by Kirkland and*
30   *Tom Fettke.]*
31   *(The stage is now covered with the greenery and decorations that*
32   *opened the program. At the close of the song, the stage explodes*
33   *in color. Christmas lights come on all over the stage. The*
34   *VILLAGERS cheer and applaud. LUMP marches Downstage*
35   *and stands on a stump. He unfurls a scroll with a proclamation.)*

1   **LUMP:**   *(Reading)* **"By order of his Majesty, King Cornelius . . .**

2   *(Looks at the audience)* **Sing!** *(Looks at the CHOIR DIRECTOR.)*

3   **Music Meister?** *(The CHOIR DIRECTOR comes On-stage and*

4   *invites the audience to stand. He or she leads them in the*

5   *"Celebration of Carols." This is a medley of familiar carols. At the*

6   *close of the carols, the CHOIR DIRECTOR seats the audience.*

7   *(Optional activity: the Grand Banner March. During this time,*

8   *KING CORNELIUS, LUMP and the VILLAGERS watch as bright*

9   *banners with the symbols of Jesus the King are processed down*

10   *the aisles. The VILLAGERS stare in awe at the beauty. A hymn*

11   *of praise toward the victorious Christ can be sung here. Suggested*

12   *song: "Lift High the Lord, Our Banner." [The original production*

13   *used the version arranged by Krogstad.] Continuing the powerful*

14   *worship of King Jesus, the VILLAGERS sing another hymn of*

15   *praise — something like "All Hail the Power of Jesus' Name." [The*

16   *original production used "All Hail King Jesus," arranged by Rhodes.])*

17   *SONG:*   "All Hail the Power of Jesus' Name."

18   **VILLAGERS:**   *(Singing)* **All hail the power of Jesus' name!**

19   **Let angels prostrate fall;**

20   **Bring forth the royal diadem,**

21   **And crown him Lord of all;**

22   **Bring forth the royal diadem,**

23   **And crown him Lord of all!**

24

25   **Ye chosen seed of Israel's race,**

26   **Ye ransomed from the fall,**

27   **Hail him who saves you by his grace,**

28   **And crown him Lord of all;**

29   **Hail him who saves you by his grace,**

30   **And crown him Lord of all!**

31

32   **Let every kindred, every tribe,**

33   **On this terrestrial ball,**

34   **To him all majesty ascribe,**

35   **And crown him Lord of all;**

1   **To him all majesty ascribe,**

2   **And crown him Lord of all!**

3

4   **O that with yonder sacred throng**

5   **We at his feet may fall!**

6   **We'll join the everlasting song,**

7   **And crown him Lord of all;**

8   **We'll join the everlasting song,**

9   **And crown him Lord of all!**

10   *(The VILLAGERS freeze. The lights put them in shadows as a*

11   *spot comes up on the trunk. GWEN, SAMMY and DAVIS come*

12   *into the square. GWEN is carrying the book. They look at all the*

13   *frozen VILLAGERS in amazement, then walk to the trunk.)*

14   **SAMMY:**   **Great story!**

15   **DAVIS:**   **Dost thou think 'twas true?** *(GWEN opens the trunk to*

16   *put the book back. She sees something.)*

17   **GWEN:**   **Friends, I think 'twas *all* true!** *(She lifts KING*

18   *CORNELIUS's crown out of the trunk and holds it up. SAMMY*

19   *and DAVIS gasp. They look up to heaven.)*

20   **GWEN, SAMMY and DAVIS:**   ***Awesome!*** *(The VILLAGERS walk*

21   *forward as the lights come up on the playing area. They sing a*

22   *final song of praise.)*

23   *SONG:*   "O Come, All Ye Faithful." *(Second verse and chorus)*

24   **VILLAGERS:**   *(Singing)* **Sing, choirs of angels,**

25   **Sing in exultation,**

26   **Sing, all ye citizens of heaven above.**

27   **Glory to God**

28   **In the highest;**

29

30   **O come, let us adore him,**

31   **O come, let us adore him,**

32   **O come, let us adore him,**

33   **Christ the Lord!**

34   *(The original production used "Glory" by Krogstad.)*

35   **EVERYONE:**   ***Merry Christmas!*** *(And the lights go to blackout.)*

THE GREAT GEMDALE
CHRISTMAS TREE ORNAMENT FACTORY

A Musical
Celebration
of the
Colors of Christmas

L. G. Enscoe
Annie Enscoe

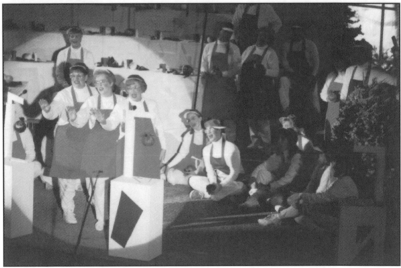

The cast of the Glendale Presbyterian production of *The Great Gemdale Christmas Tree Ornament Factory.*

THE GREAT GEMDALE
CHRISTMAS TREE ORNAMENT FACTORY

CAST

GRAMMIE

LISA and JENNY
(Two adorable little girls)

MS. PEEVISH

MR. SHRILL

CHRISTMAS STRANGER

THE GEMDALIANS (Choir)
*(Speaking parts for Gemdalians One through Eight,
and Unknown Gemdalian)*

SMALL GROUPS AND SOLOISTS (Variable)
(The original production used the following:)

SOLOIST ONE (male)

SOLOIST TWO (female)

SOLOIST THREE (either)

QUINTET

SOLOIST FOUR (either)

TRIO

RAPPERS

SOLOIST FIVE (either)

SMALL GROUP

DUET

CHORUS

CHILDREN'S TRIO

109

PRODUCTION NOTES

Running Time

Ninety minutes.

Props

Older-model radio; armchair; several children's books; Christmas tree with red and green ornaments; cardboard boxes (various sizes) — one is marked "XMAS ORNAMENTS"; ornaments in various colors; glitter; glue; spray paint; whistle; work tables; clipboard; huge rubber stamp; easel and chart; skis and poles; crèche set; Christmas lights (both red and green and multicolored); presents, including one that is especially beautifully wrapped with a tag. A crèche is inside. Cross outlined with white Christmas tree lights.

Costumes

All the Gemdalians (the Choir) are dressed in white pants, tennis shoes and turtlenecks or t-shirts. Over this goes either red or green aprons. The reverse side of the aprons are painted in a variety of colors. The aprons are then turned over to reveal a rainbow of colors at the appropriate moment. Grammie is dressed very hip. Lisa and Jenny are in pajamas.

Ms. Peevish is dressed in a sharp business outfit. (Later in the play, Ms. Peevish comes in wearing a multicolored gown.) Mr. Shrill is dressed more comically: high-water pants, a coat that had curling tails, funny glasses, big clunky shoes — sort of a cross between a nerd and that goofy man who answered Dorothy's knock on the gate at Oz.

The Christmas Stranger is dressed in ski clothes. The Soloists in the beginning wears pieces of costumes over their basic white, e.g. a sweater for "I'm Dreaming of a White Christmas," a red nose and fake antlers for "Rudolph, the Red-Nosed Reindeer," a pipe and scarf for "Frosty the Snowman," or other fitting costumes for the songs you choose.

When possible, our small group wore ethnic costumes as

they performed their songs.

Set

The set is a factory in the mountains. We built an actual factory room enclosed by stage flats painted with gizmos and gears. There were doors right and left and a big window Upstage Center. There was a long table Upstage covered in red and green ornaments. Ornaments were also hung on wires above the audience's heads. The wires were run through pulleys so the Off-stage crew could crank the ornaments back and forth across the sanctuary during the appropriate times. There is also a decorated Christmas tree.

There was a raised platform to the right of the stage (from the audience's perspective) that had a chair, table, lamp and radio. That's where Grammie, Jenny and Lisa did their scenes.

There were also small platforms of different heights to the right and left of the stage. These were used for the special singing groups — and for the comic numbers ("Frosty the Snowman," "The Grinch," etc.) that happen at the top of the program.

SUGGESTED MUSIC SOURCES

The following is information on the music used in the original production of *The Great Gemdale Christmas Tree Ornament Factory.*

There is a section in this program where ethnic Christmas music is presented. This script prints the original musical choices, but you'll want to choose music based on the ethnic make-up of your church and community.

"I'm Dreaming of a White Christmas," Irving Berlin, Irving Berlin Music Co.

"Rockin' Around the Christmas Tree," Johnny Marks, St. Nicholas Music, Inc.

"Rudolph the Red-Nosed Reindeer," Gene Autry, CPP Belwin.

"Frosty the Snowman," Steve Nelson and Jack Rollins, Chappell Music Co.

"It's the Most Wonderful Time of the Year," E. Pola and G. Wyle, arr. Hawley Ades, Shawnee Press.

"Sleigh Ride," Leroy Anderson, arr. Hawley Ades, Shawnee Press.

"Silver Bells," Jay Livingston, arr. Evans, G & W Paramount Music.

"Winter Wonderland," F. Bernard and D. Smith, Warner Bros. Music or CPP Belwin.

"Behold!", Kathie Hill and Bo Cooper, John T. Benson Publishing (Sunday Shoes Music).

"Joy to the World!" (from a musical called "Christmas People"), Geron Davis, arr. Don Marsh; PMC Publishers.

"Sing We Now of Christmas," Mark Hayes, Sparrow Music.

"Feliz Navidad" from the book *Oh, What a Love,"* by Carol Cymbala, Word Music.

"We Wish You a Merry Christmas," arr. John Hugo, Thomas House Publications.

AUTHORS' NOTES

The Great Gemdale Christmas Tree Ornament Factory is a light and warm-hearted look at the diversity of Christmas celebrations.

The script was written as a way of including a city's ethnic population into a family program and to take a lighthearted jab at the way we might hold on to only one way of celebrating Jesus' birth, when other cultures offer many and distinct additions to the holy day.

It also asks the question: "What should the church be doing at Christmas to get the gospel message out to people in a new and fresh way?"

Careful attention should be taken to getting the different small groups and soloists in and out. They should be cued up in blackouts, moving quickly from one performance to the next. This should *not* look like a talent show.

We've included the music and lyrics to the two original songs written for the evening: "The Ornament Song" and "Red and Green." Please feel free to choose your own music for the program. The songs included in this script give you an idea of theme and tone.

We used the name Gemdale for the town and Gemdalians for the factory workers. This was based on Glendale, the city of the original production. You might want to make up a humorous name based on your own city.

You have the chance to choose a representation of the ethnic community in your area. Perhaps there are even other church groups meeting in your building who can be part of this evening.

Ornaments may be distributed to members of your congregation to be brought up and placed on the tree at the appropriate time.

1   **SCENE ONE**

2   "Grammieland"

3

4   *(The program begins in darkness. Then a voice:)*

5 **VOICE:**   **Welcome, ladies and gentlemen, and thank you for**

6   **joining us for our evening of very special Christmas**

7   **music. Now, please, relax — sit back and enjoy the joyful**

8   **sounds of the holiday season.**

9   *(An elaborate musical flourish, then a spot hits SOLOIST ONE,*

10   *who is wearing a sweater and standing to the side. He starts*

11   *singing a secular Christmas song. This is some serious a cappella*

12   *Perry Como-esque crooning. Suggested song: "I'm Dreaming of*

13   *a White Christmas."*

14   *(A spotlight comes up on a radio — an older model. This shows*

15   *that the singing is coming from a radio broadcast.*

16   *(On-stage is a Christmas tree nearly trimmed with brightly*

17   *colored ornaments, a dusty cardboard box marked "XMAS*

18   *ORNAMENTS," and an overstuffed armchair.*

19   *(Our Como clone continues to warble. Just when we're beginning*

20   *to think we've come to* watch *a U.S.O. Christmas program on*

21   *radio . . . GRAMMIE comes in. She's dressed in a bathrobe and*

22   *slippers — and she's spooning from a carton of ice cream. She*

23   *looks at the radio a moment. Eats another bite. Looks at it.)*

24 **GRAMMIE:**   **I'm not in a rest home yet!** *(She turns off the station.*

25   *The SINGER freezes in mid-note. He looks around, confused by*

26   *his unseen demise. The light fades on him. GRAMMIE spins*

27   *down the dial.)* **I listen to that any longer and I'll have to**

28   **settle in for a long winter's nap . . .** *(She finds a station. A*

29   *spotlight comes up on SOLOIST TWO with a bouffant hairdo*

30   *belting out an upbeat Christmas tree song. Suggested song:*

31   *"Rockin' Around the Christmas Tree" in full Brenda Lee style.*

32   *GRAMMIE grins.)* **Hey . . . now** *that's a* **tree-trimmin' tune!**

33   *(She snaps her fingers and enjoys the beat. JENNY and LISA*

34   *laugh and shout Off-stage. GRAMMIE sighs, shouts over them.)*

35   **C'mon, girls! Let's get on in here and finish the tree. You**

1   **gotta get to sleep or Santa can't make his big delivery.**
2   *(To herself)* **Let's hope he's sitting on the roof right now**
3   **with a sack full of Sominex.** *(JENNY and LISA come bolting*
4   *in. They're dressed in p.j.s and are carrying books for GRAMMIE*
5   *to read. They've got the Christmas itch — they're jumping up and*
6   *down and laughing.)*
7   LISA: **My turn to put an ornament on!**
8   JENNY: **Get lost, dorky! It's my turn.**
9   GRAMMIE: **All right, each of you gets to put one more bulb on**
10   **the tree, and then you hit the hay. So, pick one.** *(They go*
11   *to a box and look in.)*
12   LISA: **I want the green bulb.**
13   JENNY: **I want the red one.**
14   LISA: **I want the red one!**
15   JENNY: **You just said —**
16   GRAMMIE: **Lisa, green. Jenny, red. Now get your bulbs in**
17   **gear.** *(They give each other a look and pick up red and green*
18   *bulbs. They go to the tree and carefully hang them. They admire*
19   *the tree for a moment.)* **It's very beautiful, girls.**
20   LISA: **Grammie, why do we have Christmas trees at Christmas?**
21   GRAMMIE: **I think it's because . . . Grammie doesn't remember,**
22   **honey. Always been like that, I guess. I do know there's**
23   **something very important about a tree this time of year.**
24   *(They look at the tree a moment more.)* **OK, girls! Tree trimmin'**
25   **is officially over. Let's head for the sack.** *(GRAMMIE turns*
26   *off the radio. The SINGER freezes in mid-note. Looks around*
27   *for the invisible source of her doom. The spotlight goes out.)*
28   JENNY: **C'mon, Grammie! Tuck us into bed!**
29   LISA: **Tuck us in so morning'll get here fast!**
30   JENNY: **Tuck us in!**
31   GRAMMIE: **Hey, wait a minute . . . why can't we tuck**
32   **Grammie in for once?** *(JENNY and LISA stop. They stare at*
33   *her, confused.)*
34   LISA: **But you hafta tuck *us* in.**
35   GRAMMIE: **Where does it say Grammies *always* have to do**

1   **the tucking, huh? Is it in a book somewhere? "Grammie's**
2   **Book of Gottas"? Why can't Grammies get tucked in once**
3   **in a while?**
4   **JENNY:**   **But Mom always tucks us in!** *Always.*
5   **GRAMMIE:**   **Well, unfortunately your mom had to work**
6   **tonight and you girls ended up in Grammieland for**
7   **Christmas Eve. And here in Grammieland — Grammie**
8   **makes up the rules.**
9   **JENNY:**   **OK, then how about reading us a Christmas story.**
10   **Huh? Is that allowed in Grammieland? Is it?**
11   **GRAMMIE:**   **Grammie doesn't like to read stories.**
12   **LISA:**   **Grammie, don't play that.**
13   **JENNY:**   **C'mon, Grams. Something? Anything?**
14   **GRAMMIE:**   *(Pause, then relenting)* **Let me see what books**
15   **you've got there.** *(GRAMMIE takes the stack of books and sits*
16   *in the easy chair. She picks the top book and opens it. A spotlight*
17   *hits SOLOIST THREE, who is wearing a red nose and fake*
18   *antlers. He/she starts warbling. Suggested song: "Rudolph, the*
19   *Red-Nosed Reindeer." GRAMMIE slams the book closed. The*
20   *spotlight snaps off SOLOIST THREE.)*
21   **Can't you find another story, honey? Grammie must**
22   **have read "Rudolph"** *(Or whatever song you choose)* **to your**
23   **mother half a million times. I was sure glad when it came**
24   **on TV and she could just watch it.**
25   **JENNY:**   **Try the next one.** *(GRAMMIE picks up the next book.*
26   *She opens it. A spotlight picks up a QUINTET singing the "Fa-*
27   *hoo Fo-ray" song from* How the Grinch Stole Christmas.
28   *GRAMMIE slams the book closed. The spotlight snaps off the*
29   *QUINTET.)*
30   **GRAMMIE:**   **Grammie never** *could* **read the** *Grinch,* **honey.**
31   **She gets tongue-tied. Let's try one more.** *(GRAMMIE picks*
32   *up another book. She opens it. A spotlight hits SOLOIST FOUR*
33   *singing very animatedly and wearing a pipe and scarf. Suggested*
34   *song: "Frosty the Snowman." GRAMMIE slams the book. The*
35   *spotlight snaps off SOLOIST FOUR. GRAMMIE shudders.)*

1   Honey, Frosty always gave Grammie the willies. Those
2   coal-black eyes.
3 JENNY: C'mon, Grams, we need a story to help us fall asleep.
4 LISA: Yeah, we have insominex.
5 GRAMMIE: All right . . . we'll have a story. But not one of
6   these. *(She thinks a moment.)* **OK, I guess Grammie's gonna**
7   **have to make up a story.**
8 JENNY: This isn't going to be another Walking-Ten-Miles-
9   to-School-in-the-Snow-With-Alligators kinda story, is it?
10 GRAMMIE: Wait a minute. There really were alligators.
11 LISA: In Seattle?
12 GRAMMIE: Grammie had to walk right past the aquarium on
13   her way to school *every* morning. Anyway, I want to tell
14   a *Christmas* story. *(She throws her arms open.)* **Come on,**
15   **girls. Sit next to Grammie, and she'll tell you all about**
16   **the little teeny tiny town known as** . . . *(Thinking)*
17   . . . **Gemdale.** *(JENNY and LISA snuggle in.)* **Now, the town**
18   **of Gemdale was so teeny-tiny, they only had *one* mall.**
19 LISA: No way . . .
20 GRAMMIE: And Gemdale was so high up in the mountains,
21   it was always snowing. All year 'round. But it was a thick,
22   slushy kind of pack, you know. Not really good for skiing.
23   So no one ever went up there. Now . . . *(Where does she go*
24   *with it?)* . . . **ah, in the middle of this town there was**
25   **a** . . . **big factory. It was** . . . *(She sees the "XMAS*
26   *ORNAMENTS" box.)* . . . **an ornament factory! That's it. An**
27   **ornament factory where they made the ornaments for**
28   **the whole world! It was called** . . . *The Great Gemdale*
29   *Christmas Tree Ornament Factory!* *(The lights go out on*
30   *GRAMMIE, LISA and JENNY.)*
31
32
33
34
35

1   **SCENE TWO**

2   "Gemdale"

3

4   *(Lights come up on the sanctuary platform revealing the Gemdale*

5   *Christmas Tree Ornament Factory. The CHOIR [hereafter*

6   *known as GEMDALIANS] is cheerfully bustling in ornament-*

7   *making vignettes: gluing, glittering, painting, wiring. Several*

8   *are acting as quality control. Some are counting products. The*

9   *scene looks thriving.*

10   *(Work tables are set up all over covered with wire, paper, glitter,*

11   *spray paint — all the things to make ornaments. In the Upstage*

12   *Center of the room, there's a huge window frame — outside, snow-*

13   *covered trees can be seen. There's a decorated Christmas tree.*

14   *(Right, there are stacks of huge plain-wrapped packaged boxes*

15   *with addresses of city names from all over the country. A sign,*

16   *SHIPPING/RECEIVING, hangs above them. The boxes are*

17   *stacked to make levels for GEMDALIANS. [NOTE: There are*

18   *several other levels around the sanctuary where SOLOISTS will*

19   *be lit by spotlights.]*

20   *(The audience will quickly notice that everything is red and green.*

21   *The ornaments being made are all red and green. The bulbs on*

22   *the tree are red and green. Even the GEMDALIANS are dressed*

23   *only in shades of red and green!*

24   *(At lights, the GEMDALIANS are singing their "Ornament*

25   *Song." [The original production used a snappy, whistle-while-*

26   *you-work kind of tune for these lyrics.])*

27 **SONG:**   "Ornament Song." (What We Hang on the Tree) *(See music,*

28   *page 142.)*

29 **GEMDALIANS:**   *(Singing)* **Glitter, glue, some paint, too,**

30   **All goes in the sparkling stew**

31   **To make our tree-bright ornaments**

32   **That gleam and shine and make you "Ooo!"**

33

34   **Bulbs, stars, angels fly,**

35   **Shapes you all must recognize,**

1   They shout: "Look! Christmas is here!"
2   To all the cheerful passers-by!
3 *CHORUS:*   What we hang on the tree is beautiful!
4   On the tree, beautiful!
5   It makes Christmas wonderful,
6   What we see hanging on the tree!
7   *(Repeat CHORUS.)*
8   *(The "Ornament Song" ends. The GEMDALIANS freeze. The*
9   *lights fade on them. Bright music plays in the darkness.)*
10
11
12
13
14
15
16
17
18
19
20
21
22
23
24
25
26
27
28
29
30
31
32
33
34
35

1	**SCENE THREE**
2	"Grammieland"
3	
4	*(The lights come up on GRAMMIE, JENNY and LISA as*
5	*GRAMMIE continues the story.)*
6	**JENNY:** That's all they made? Christmas ornaments?
7	**LISA:** Yeah. That's it?
8	**GRAMMIE:** That's all they made. Christmas ornaments. All
9	year 'round — bulbs, bells, balls. Each and every one of
10	the Gemdalians just loved Christmas and making
11	Christmas tree ornaments — especially this time of year
12	when Christmas was just around the corner. Day and
13	night, they grinned as they glittered and glued, painted
14	and packed! And they sang. Sang, sang, sang. Summer,
15	fall, winter and spring! And as a result, the company's
16	employee turnover was almost nil, their HMO claims
17	were very low, and the Human Resources Department
18	was nearly empty of complaints. *(JENNY and LISA shoot*
19	*a "Hunh?" look at each other. The lights black out on them.)*
20	
21	
22	
23	
24	
25	
26	
27	
28	
29	
30	
31	
32	
33	
34	
35	

121

1	<div align="center">**SCENE FOUR**</div>
2	<div align="center">"Gemdale"</div>
3	
4	*(The lights come up on the factory. The GEMDALIANS are*
5	*grinning, making ornaments and singing. Suggested song: "It's*
6	*the Most Wonderful Time of the Year."*
7	*(Following the song, sleigh bells ring from Off-stage. One of the*
8	*GEMDALIANS runs to the "window" and looks out. [These*
9	*segues should all be a little tongue-in-cheek.])*
10	**GEMDALIAN ONE:** *(Waving to someone outside)* **Hey, everybody!**
11	**Frank Johnson just went by in his sleigh headin' into**
12	**town! Hi ya, Frank!**
13	**ALL GEMDALIANS: Hi ya, Frank!**
14	*(Suggested song: "Sleigh Ride.")*
15	**GEMDALIAN TWO: Maxine! Laverne! Patty! Sing us one of**
16	**your favorites!** *(A TRIO dashes forward and sings. Suggested*
17	*Song: "Silver Bells." The GEMDALIANS freeze. The lights come*
18	*up on GRAMMIE, JENNY and LISA. GRAMMIE leans*
19	*forward, getting ready to continue her story.)*
20	**GRAMMIE: Oh, those Gemdalians sure loved to sing!**
21	**Morning, noon, and night. But as we'll soon find out —**
22	*(The GEMDALIANS suddenly launch into another song. The*
23	*lights fade on GRAMMIE, JENNY and LISA as they stare at*
24	*the GEMDALIANS in amazement for cutting in. Suggested song:*
25	*"Winter Wonderland."*
26	*(The GEMDALIANS finish the song frozen in Currier & Ives*
27	*vignettes — laughing, hugging, shaking hands, exchanging*
28	*presents, waving at each other, etc. It's truly a winter*
29	*wonderland.)*
30	
31	
32	
33	
34	
35	

1 **SCENE FIVE**
2 "Grammieland"
3
4 *(The lights come up on GRAMMIE, JENNY and LISA. They*
5 *look bored. LISA is fighting off sleep.)*
6 **JENNY: Wow, they sure can sing a lot, can't they Grammie?**
7 **LISA:** *(Yawning)* **Yeah . . . a lot.**
8 **GRAMMIE:** *(Looking at the GEMDALIANS)* **It's a wonder they**
9   **get any ornaments made at all!** *(The lights fade on the*
10   *GEMDALIANS as they smile and wave mischeviously at*
11   *GRAMMIE.)* **But things weren't all wonderland and sleigh**
12   **rides over at the Great Gemdale Christmas Tree**
13   **Ornament Factory. A big problem was about to take the**
14   **jingle out of their ring-ting-tingle. You see, the**
15   **Gemdalians had been making the same Christmas**
16   **ornaments in the same way since, well, before**
17   **Eisenhower was in office.**
18 **LISA: Who?**
19 **GRAMMIE: You know . . . Ike. He's a hit with a mike.**
20 **JENNY: Ike?**
21 **GRAMMIE: All right! They've been making the same**
22   **Christmas ornaments in the same way since before there**
23   **was MTV.**
24 **JENNY:** *Wowww!* **A million years ago.**
25 **GRAMMIE: Totally. And the Gemdalians were about to find**
26   **out what a different world it was beyond their snowy**
27   **white factory walls.** *(The lights come down on GRAMMIE,*
28   *JENNY and LISA.)*
29
30
31
32
33
34
35

1	**SCENE SIX**
2	"Gemdale"
3	
4	*(Lights up on the GEMDALIANS — in the same frozen Currier*
5	*& Ives vignettes. One of them looks off down the aisle. He starts*
6	*quivering.)*
7	**GEMDALIAN THREE:** It's Ms. Peevish!
8	**GEMDALIAN ONE:** And Mr. Shrill! *(The GEMDALIANS*
9	*scramble back to their work stations, bumping into each other*
10	*along the way. They start singing the "Ornament Song." See*
11	*music, page 142.*
12	*(MS. PEEVISH, the owner of the Gemdale Christmas Tree*
13	*Ornament Factory, stalks onto the stage. She's all business,*
14	*looking like a realtor caricature in her red blazer and green skirt.*
15	*She carries official-looking material. MR. SHRILL, her squirrely*
16	*assistant, shuffles in behind her. He has a huge rubber stamp.*
17	*She waits for the GEMDALIANS to stop singing. They don't.*
18	*They're ignoring her.)*
19	**PEEVISH:** *(Clears her throat.)* **Excuse me ... people! People!**
20	**Excuse me. I said *excuse* me!** *(PEEVISH nods at SHRILL,*
21	*who blows a very shrill whistle. The GEMDALIANS stop*
22	*singing. They notice her.)*
23	**ALL GEMDALIANS:** *(The old classroom drill)* **Merry Christmas,**
24	**Ms. Peevish.**
25	**PEEVISH:** **Thank you. Now, people, I'm afraid I have some**
26	**very bad news for you all. News that could very well**
27	**affect the future of Gemdale and all you fine, hard-**
28	**working ornament engineers.**
29	**GEMDALIAN FOUR:** **Are you canceling the Christmas party**
30	**again?**
31	**PEEVISH:** **I'm afraid it's worse than that.**
32	**GEMDALIAN FIVE:** **The vending machines are out of M & Ms**
33	**again?**
34	**GEMDALIAN SIX:** **The red and green kind?!**
35	**PEEVISH:** **No, no, it's much, much —**

1 GEMDALIAN SEVEN: You're not gonna sing "O Tannenbaum"
2   a cappella again, are you?
3 PEEVISH: You all said you loved that last year! But that's
4   not the bad news. Mr. Shrill! Give 'em the bad news!
5   *(SHRILL scrambles over to the addressed packages and begins*
6   *to stamp all of them "Canceled." The GEMDALIANS are in*
7   *shock. They gesture, throw up their hands, babble at each other,*
8   *shake their heads.)* That's right! "Canceled! Canceled!
9   Canceled!" All our orders canceled! Nobody wants to buy
10   Gemdale's ornaments — and you know why? Because
11   they say we're too old-fashioned! Too backward! *Too*
12   *nonprogressive!* Give 'em the spiel, Mr. Shrill! *(SHRILL*
13   *sets up an easel and a huge green chart sporting a downward*
14   *climbing red line. It spans 1894 to 1994.)*
15 SHRILL: *(A confusing ramble in a reedy, nasal voice)* The product
16   ratio of incoming units going out with double-truck
17   advertising and decreasing points on the amortized
18   listing of units unsold in liquid assets and outstanding
19   deficits given our current AMEX stature and low-profile
20   consumer interest is final, ipso facto proof that . . . well,
21   nobody's buyin' our doodads.
22 PEEVISH: *(Rolling her eyes)* Thank you, Shrill.
23 SHRILL: You betcha, Peevish.
24 GEMDALIAN SEVEN: But we've been making ornaments
25   the same way for a hundred years!
26 GEMDALIAN THREE: We've always done it this way!
27 GEMDALIAN FIVE: Red and green! Red and green!
28 ALL GEMDALIANS: People just love red and green!
29 PEEVISH: Obviously not, glitterheads! Things must be
30   changing out there and we don't know about it! *And I*
31   *loathe being left out!*
32 UNKNOWN GEMDALIAN: Why don't we send someone to
33   see what it's like out there?
34 PEEVISH: Who said that? *(No one speaks; no one moves.)* C'mon,
35   who said that? Well, I think it's an excellent idea. Any

125

1   **volunteers? Anyone want to leave the safety of the factory**
2   **grounds and do a little on-site research?** *(No one speaks;*
3   *no one moves.)* **Just as I thought! Well, it doesn't matter,**
4   **because you're *still* going to have to come up with new**
5   **ornament ideas! We need some brand-spanking new**
6   **product ventures for the new Christmas tree ornament**
7   **market!**
8   **GEMDALIAN FIVE:**   **More red ornaments!**
9   **GEMDALIAN TWO:**   **More green ornaments!**
10   **RED GEMDALIANS:**   *Red!*
11   **GREEN GEMDALIANS:**   *Green! (They start shouting at each*
12   *other: "Red!" "Green!" PEEVISH nods at SHRILL, who blows*
13   *a shrill whistle. The GEMDALIANS shush and look at her.)*
14   **PEEVISH:**   **Christmas Eve! You have until *Christmas Eve* to**
15   **come up with new ornaments! Or on Christmas Day**
16   **you're all gonna see a big, fat board across these factory**
17   **doors! And you can all go home to Christmas dinners of**
18   **roasted walking papers and cranberried unemployment**
19   **lines!** *(SHRILL blows his shrill whistle for emphasis. PEEVISH*
20   *and SHRILL turn on their heels and stomp out. The*
21   *GEMDALIANS turn to each other in consternation. The music*
22   *reflects this, which gradually builds into the song "Red and*
23   *Green." See music, page 144.)*
24   *SONG:*   "Red and Green."
25   **GEMDALIANS:**   *(Singing)* **Red and green, red and green,**
26   **Isn't that what Christmas means?**
27   **Hang a wreath on the old front door,**
28   **Scatterings of gifts across the floor.**
29   **Isn't that what Christmas means?**
30
31   **Green and red, green and red,**
32   **Isn't that what the season said?**
33   **Smile and greet and shake a hand,**
34   **A familiar tune from the Christmas band.**
35   **Isn't that what the season spreads?**

1   What more do we need
2   To give us all Godspeed
3   And a warm glow glowing inside?
4   What more do we lack
5   To put each one on track
6   To yuletide memories long ago back?
7
8   Red and green, red and green,
9   The prettiest colors we've ever seen.
10 Who could ask for something more
11 To brighten up the home or store?
12 Isn't that our holiday scene?
13
14 Green and red, green and red,
15 Rainbow colors in our heads.
16 Why change the horse in midstream?
17 Just what is the holiday theme?
18 Is there more left unsaid?
19
20 Red and green, red and green
21 Isn't that what Christmas means?
22 *(The lights fade on the GEMDALIANS in a sad state.)*
23
24
25
26
27
28
29
30
31
32
33
34
35

1	**SCENE SEVEN**
2	"Grammieland"
3	
4	*(The lights come up on GRAMMIE, JENNY and LISA. JENNY*
5	*and LISA are really into the story.)*
6	**JENNY:** What're they gonna do, Grammie?
7	**LISA:** Yeah, who's gonna help 'em out?
8	**GRAMMIE:** You know, girls, sometimes when you've got a
9	problem, it takes somebody from the outside to help you
10	figure it out.
11	**LISA:** Like when Mom taught me how to tie my shoes 'cause I
12	had no idea how two stupid strings made a together knot?
13	**GRAMMIE:** Exactly. Well, that somebody came one cold
14	winter's night just before Christmas Eve. Nobody knew
15	his name. Nobody knew what he did. Nobody knew where
16	he came from. But there he was! Like he dropped out of
17	the sky! And he had something to say to the Gemdalians.
18	He told them something they didn't know — *and*
19	something they had long forgotten. Something that
20	would change the Gemdalians forever and ever.
21	**LISA:** Amen. *(GRAMMIE looks at LISA and smiles. The lights*
22	*fade on GRAMMIE, JENNY and LISA.)*
23	
24	
25	
26	
27	
28	
29	
30	
31	
32	
33	
34	
35	

1   **SCENE EIGHT**

2   "Gemdale"

3

4   *(In the darkness, the loud sound of a crash is heard. The lights*

5   *come up on the factory. Someone dressed in ski clothes and dusted*

6   *with snow is piled in the middle of the factory. He's a tangle of*

7   *skis, poles and equipment. It looks like he came off a slope right*

8   *through the factory doors and wiped out. He stands. This is the*

9   *CHRISTMAS STRANGER. The GEMDALIANS are staring*

10   *aghast at him, as if he dropped out of the sky.)*

11 **CHRISTMAS STRANGER:**   Hi. *(Nobody says anything.)* **Oh.**

12   **Uh . . . sorry for dropping in on you like this. I**

13   **was . . . uh . . . skiing up the hill over there and I . . . well,**

14   **I sorta missed the bottom of the slope and kept going.**

15   **Ended up here.** *(Nobody says anything.)* **Did you know you**

16   **guys don't exist? I mean, I didn't see you on my Triple A**

17   **map . . .**

18 **GEMDALIAN ONE:**   Somebody from the outside!

19 **GEMDALIAN FOUR:**   Maybe he can help us!

20 **GEMDALIAN EIGHT:**   Tell us what Christmas is like out

21   there!

22 **CHRISTMAS STRANGER:**   Out where?

23 **ALL GEMDALIANS:**   Out there!

24 **CHRISTMAS STRANGER:**   *(Looks out the window.)* **You mean,**

25   **like, out in** _____ *(Your city here)* **or something?**

26   *(Looks around.)* **Hey, you're . . . you're making ornaments**

27   **here, aren't you?** *(Hits him.)* **Wait a minute . . . these are**

28   **Gemdale Christmas tree ornaments! Of course. So this is**

29   **where you make 'em, huh? The Great Gemdale Christmas**

30   **Tree Ornament Factory. Gee, I haven't bought a Gemdale**

31   **ornament in years.**

32 **PEEVISH:**   And why not, Christmas Stranger? *(PEEVISH and*

33   *SHRILL are suddenly there, standing in the aisle. The*

34   *GEMDALIANS whisper among themselves.)*

35 **CHRISTMAS STRANGER:**   Well, I don't know . . . I guess

1	there are just so many, you know, interesting and vibrant
2	colors and designs out there now. You guys're,
3	well . . . you're kinda boring. I mean, I don't know if you
4	guys've noticed, but everything you make here is either
5	red or green.
6	ALL GEMDALIANS: What's wrong with red and green?!
7	CHRISTMAS STRANGER: *(Startled)* Oh! Well, nothing, I
8	guess . . . other than the fact that it shows a rather timidly
9	traditional, unimaginative design sense. I mean, it's
10	kinda like singing only "Jingle Bells" and "Deck the
11	Halls" the whole season, isn't it? People out there want
12	more.
13	SHRILL: OK, Mr. Smarty Pants Christmas Stranger Who
14	Dropped on Us Out of Nowhere, maybe you can tell us
15	exactly what people *do* want out there.
16	CHRISTMAS STRANGER: That sounds like a cue to me.
17	SHRILL: So what if it is?
18	CHRISTMAS STRANGER: Well, the first thing people want —
19	but not everybody knows it — is to hear the Christmas
20	story.
21	GEMDALIAN THREE: The *what?*
22	CHRISTMAS STRANGER: The Christmas story. You know,
23	Bethlehem, the angels, the baby in the manger . . . *(Sings.)*
24	"We three kings . . ." *(He's looking at a spate of blank faces.)*
25	I don't understand. What do you think the Christmas
26	ornaments are all about?
27	GEMDALIAN THREE: Christmas wouldn't be Christmas
28	without somethin' hangin' on a tree!
29	CHRISTMAS STRANGER: You're right. *(He smiles.)* You want
30	to know what it's like out there. I'll tell you. I was standing
31	on a corner yesterday in the town I live in *(Or your city*
32	*here)* and I could hear the Christmas story all around me.
33	It sounded like this.
34	*(At this point, the original production represented the ethnic*
35	*make-up of the community by bringing in cameo musical*

1   *performances by a variety of ethnic choirs, choruses and soloists.*
2   *[This script will offer the ethnic choices of the original*
3   *production.]*
4   *(A rap beat kicks in. The lights pick up some RAPPERS on a*
5   *platform. They sing a song about the angels appearing to the*
6   *shepherds. [The original production used "Behold!" by Cooper.]*
7   *By the end of the song, the GEMDALIANS have joined in by*
8   *moving, smiling, clapping.)*
9   **CHRISTMAS STRANGER:**   **And I could hear something else.**
10   **I turned around, and from a small shop window across**
11   **the street, I heard the sound of a voice.** *(The light comes*
12   *up on SOLOIST FIVE singing about Jesus in the manger. [The*
13   *original production used a version of "What Child Is This?" sung*
14   *in Korean by a Korean soloist in traditional costume.])*
15   *SONG:*   "What Child Is This?" (Verses 1 and 3)
16   **SOLOIST FIVE:**   *(Singing)* **What child is this, who, laid to rest**
17   **On Mary's lap is sleeping?**
18   **Whom angels greet with anthems sweet,**
19   **While shepherds watch are keeping?**
20
21   **This, this is Christ the King,**
22   **Whom shepherds guard and angels sing:**
23   **Haste, haste to bring him laud,**
24   **The babe, the son of Mary!**
25
26   **So bring him incense, gold and myrrh,**
27   **Come, peasant, king, to own him,**
28   **The King of kings salvation brings,**
29   **Let loving hearts enthrone him.**
30
31   **This, this is Christ the King,**
32   **Whom shepherds guard and angels sing:**
33   **Haste, haste to bring him laud,**
34   **The babe, the son of Mary!**
35   *(The lights come down on SOLOIST FIVE.)*

1   **CHRISTMAS STRANGER:**   **I passed by a restaurant. It wasn't**
2   **open yet, but I could hear the workers inside. I don't**
3   **know how many people there were, but it sounded like**
4   **a heavenly choir. I stopped at the door to listen.** *(A*
5   *spotlight picks up a SMALL GROUP. They sing "O Little Town*
6   *of Bethlehem." [The original production used a Hispanic choir*
7   *dressed in bright colors and singing in Spanish.])*
8   ***SONG:***   "O Little Town of Bethlehem."
9   **SMALL GROUP:**   *(Singing)* **O little town of Bethlehem!**
10   **How still we see thee lie;**
11   **Above thy deep and dreamless sleep,**
12   **The silent stars go by.**
13
14   **Yet in thy dark streets shineth**
15   **The everlasting Light;**
16   **The hopes and fears of all the years**
17   **Are met in thee tonight.**
18
19   **For Christ is born of Mary;**
20   **And gathered all above,**
21   **While mortals sleep, the angels keep**
22   **Their watch of wond'ring love.**
23
24   **O morning stars, together**
25   **Proclaim the holy birth;**
26   **And praises sing to God the King,**
27   **And peace to all on earth.**
28
29   **How silently, how silently,**
30   **The wondrous gift is giv'n!**
31   **So God imparts to human hearts**
32   **The blessings of his heav'n.**
33
34   **No ear may hear his coming;**
35   **But in this world of sin,**

1   Where meek souls will receive him still,
2   The dear Christ enters in.
3
4   O holy child of Bethlehem!
5   Descend on us, we pray,
6   Cast out our sins and enter in,
7   Be born in us today.
8
9   We hear the Christmas angels
10   The great glad tidings tell,
11   Oh, come to us, abide with us,
12   Our Lord, Emmanuel!
13   *(The lights come down on the SMALL GROUP. The*
14   *CHRISTMAS STRANGER turns to the GEMDALIANS. They*
15   *are absolutely lost in the music.)*
16   CHRISTMAS STRANGER: Any of this starting to sound
17   familiar?
18   GEMDALIAN ONE: I recognize that tune! I've heard it
19   before, I know I have.
20   GEMDALIAN SIX: I've been in here painting ornaments for
21   so long, I forgot about the Christmas story.
22   GEMDALIAN FOUR: And I like all those colors they're
23   wearing.
24   PEEVISH: I don't see what any of this has to do with
25   marketing ornaments. We need new *ideas!*
26   SHRILL: We need to sell, sell, sell!
27   CHRISTMAS STRANGER: What I'm telling you has nothing
28   to do with marketing ornaments. And everything. Can I
29   tell you some more?
30   ALL GEMDALIANS: Please, sir, can we have some more?
31   CHRISTMAS STRANGER: OK. OK, that's great. Well, I
32   started walking down the street. I heard these beautiful
33   voices coming from an apartment window above me. I
34   stopped to listen. *(The spotlight picks up a DUET singing a*
35   *carol about the angel Gabriel visiting Mary. [The original*

1   *production used "Salaam (Peace to the World)," a Jordanian*
2   *carol sung by two Jordanian men in traditional costume.] The*
3   *lights come down on the DUET. The CHRISTMAS STRANGER*
4   *looks at the GEMDALIANS. They are delighted with the music.)*

5   **CHRISTMAS STRANGER: Well, I kept walking. I was**
6   **passing a park when I saw a group of families standing**
7   **around a bench. While I watched, they started singing to**
8   **each other. I stood there in the cold. I couldn't move. And**
9   **I listened.**

10   *(The lights pick up a CHORUS. They sing a song about the*
11   *revelation of Jesus to the world. [The original production offered*
12   *an Armenian church choir singing "Krisdos EE Mcch*
13   *(Revelation of Jesus)" by A. Yegmalian.]*
14   *(The lights come down on the CHORUS, and come up on a*
15   *CHILDREN'S TRIO. They sing a lullaby song to the Christ*
16   *child. [The original production used "Shaio Bao-Bao" by Hodges*
17   *and sung by three Chinese girls.]*
18   *(The lights come down on the CHILDREN'S TRIO. The*
19   *CHRISTMAS STRANGER with his eyes closed, is lost in the*
20   *haunting melody. He repeats the chorus in English. Finally he*
21   *opens his eyes and looks at the GEMDALIANS.)*

22   **CHRISTMAS STRANGER:** *(Softly)* **Don't you see? Red and**
23   **green isn't enough. It's not nearly enough.** *(Excited again)*
24   **OK. So, I walked on. I passed this little church on the**
25   **corner. There were a million people stuffed inside. So**
26   **many people, they had to open the doors to let air in.**
27   **And they were singing this:** *(Suddenly the GEMDALIANS*
28   *break into an African-American gospel version of "Joy to the*
29   *World!" It surprises the CHRISTMAS STRANGER. Then he*
30   *smiles. [The original production used a version by Davis,*
31   *arranged by Marsh.])*

32   *SONG:* "Joy to the World!"
33   **GEMDALIANS:** *(Singing)* **Joy to the world!**
34   **Oh, joy to the world!**
35   **The Lord is come**

1   **Let earth receive her King!**

2

3   **Let ev'ry heart prepare him room,**

4   **And heav'n and nature sing,**

5   **And heav'n and nature sing,**

6   **And heav'n and nature sing . . .**

7   *(The GEMDALIANS are obviously excited now. The stage can*

8   *hardly contain them.)*

9   CHRISTMAS STRANGER: Well, that's it. That's what

10   Christmas is like out there.

11   PEEVISH: That's a wonderful story, pal. But we need ideas

12   about *ornaments*. People just aren't buying the way we

13   do things anymore.

14   CHRISTMAS STRANGER: You're right about that.

15   PEEVISH: And no matter what you say, people *still* need to

16   see something hanging on the tree. Catch our drift?

17   CHRISTMAS STRANGER: You don't know how true that is.

18   SHRILL: What's that supposed to mean, inscrutable stranger?

19   CHRISTMAS STRANGER: Don't you see? What you make

20   here should remind everybody what Christmas is all

21   about!

22   PEEVISH: That's exactly what we've been doing for one

23   hundred years!

24   CHRISTMAS STRANGER: It seems to me you've been telling

25   people *what* to hang on a tree.

26   PEEVISH: That's our motto!

27   CHRISTMAS STRANGER: *(After a moment)* **Why don't you try**

28   **telling people about *who* hung on the tree?** *(Everyone stops.*

29   *Dead silence.)* **The most priceless treasure a tree has ever**

30   **had the pleasure of holding.** *(The SMALL GROUPS and*

31   *SOLOISTS start coming down the aisles while the CHRISTMAS*

32   *STRANGER speaks. They fill the stage with the colors of their*

33   *costumes. CHRISTMAS STRANGER continues.)* **Jesus Christ**

34   **was hung on the first Christmas tree. The cross on**

35   **Calvary. He was the only weight that tree could bear. And**

1   **it was a colorful tree. The colors of the whole world were**
2   **up there with him.** *(Pauses.)* **Jesus is what your ornaments**
3   **are all about. And his tree is the most beautiful. More**
4   **beautiful than any Christmas tree this world has ever**
5   **seen. Just take a look.**
6   *(Suddenly the lights go to black. White lights outlining a cross*
7   *suspended over the set come up full. The cross hangs in the dark,*
8   *cool air for a moment. Then the lights come up. The CHRISTMAS*
9   *STRANGER is gone. In his place is a beautiful, colorfully*
10   *wrapped present. Everyone looks around. They whisper in*
11   *amazement. PEEVISH walks to the box. She looks at the tag.)*
12   **PEEVISH:** *(Amazed)* **It's for us ...** *(PEEVISH opens it. The*
13   *GEMDALIANS strain forward to see. She pulls something out*
14   *of the box. It's a beautiful crèche scene. The GEMDALIANS*
15   *freeze. The lights fade on the factory. In the darkness, the*
16   *GEMDALIANS reverse their aprons so the brightly colored side*
17   *is in front. A light comes up on GRAMMIE, JENNY and LISA,*
18   *whose faces are rapt with attention.*
19   **GRAMMIE:**   **And that's what finally saved the Great Gemdale**
20   **Christmas Tree Ornament Factory from going under. The**
21   **Gemdalians saw the light — and it was a Christmas**
22   **rainbow!**
23   **JENNY:**   **I love rainbows!**
24   **LISA:**   **Yeah,** *all* **the colors of the** *rainbow!*
25   *(The lights come up on the factory. The GEMDALIANS unfreeze*
26   *and look at themselves in amazement. Their red or green aprons*
27   *have become a whole Crayola crayon box of colors! PEEVISH is*
28   *gone. SHRILL is very upset. But from behind the GEMDALIANS,*
29   *someone is coming toward the front of the stage. The*
30   *GEMDALIANS part, whispering among themselves in*
31   *amazement. It's PEEVISH. And she's dressed in a gorgeous gown*
32   *full of the colors of the rainbow.)*
33   **PEEVISH:**   **I want to see new colors!**
34   **SHRILL:**   **And new designs!**
35   **RED GEMDALIANS:**   **Red!**

1 **GREEN GEMDALIANS: Green!** *(They look at each other. Is it*
2 *going to be the same war?)*
3 **GEMDALIAN ONE: Blue!**
4 **GEMDALIAN TWO: Yellow!**
5 **GEMDALIAN THREE: Brown!**
6 **GEMDALIAN FOUR: Purple!**
7 **GEMDALIAN FIVE: Gold!**
8 **GEMDALIAN SIX: *Fuuuschiaaa!***
9 **GEMDALIAN SEVEN: And how about a nice taupey kind of a**
10 **drab olive with just a hint of hazelnut kind of thing.** *(The*
11 *GEMDALIANS launch into a festive song about Christmas.*
12 *Suggested song: "Sing We Now of Christmas." PEEVISH and*
13 *SHRILL join in. The SOLOISTS and SMALL GROUPS join*
14 *in. The GEMDALIANS start redecorating the Christmas tree as*
15 *they sing.*
16 *(By the end of the song, the Christmas tree has become a new*
17 *creation, with bright colors and bulbs. [But the tree lights aren't*
18 *plugged in yet.] PEEVISH admires the tree. There's a space in*
19 *the middle of the branches where no one has hung ornaments.*
20 *She picks up the crèche and sets it in the middle of the tree.*
21 *PEEVISH begins "Hark, the Herald Angels Sing!" a cappella.*
22 *The GEMDALIANS, SOLOISTS and SMALL GROUPS join*
23 *in. They encourage the congregation to sing and bring up*
24 *ornaments to place on the tree. Everyone sings a selection of*
25 *familiar carols: "Hark, the Herald Angels Sing!", "The First*
26 *Noel," "O Come, All Ye Faithful," "Silent Night." At the end of*
27 *"Silent Night," the lights come down low. There's a moment of*
28 *silence.)*
29
30
31
32
33
34
35

1	**SCENE NINE**
2	"Grammieland"
3	
4	*(The lights come up slowly on GRAMMIE, JENNY and LISA.*
5	*GRAMMIE has fallen asleep, and JENNY and LISA are staring*
6	*at her.)*
7	**LISA:** I guess the excitement was too much for her.
8	**JENNY:** We can't leave it here. Let's finish the story.
9	**LISA:** It sounds finished to me.
10	**JENNY:** No, we need a grand finale!
11	**LISA:** A what?
12	**JENNY:** Like this: "And then the room was filled with happy,
13	joyful Gemdalians, and they sang, sang, sang. Day and
14	night. Winter, spring, summer and fall! But most
15	especially at Christmas time!" *(The lights go out on*
16	*GRAMMIE, JENNY and LISA.)*
17	
18	
19	
20	
21	
22	
23	
24	
25	
26	
27	
28	
29	
30	
31	
32	
33	
34	
35	

1	**SCENE TEN**
2	"Gemdale"
3	
4	*(The lights come up on the factory. The GEMDALIANS, SMALL*
5	*GROUPS and SOLOISTS break into a song celebrating the*
6	*different colors and customs of Christmas. Suggested song: "Feliz*
7	*Navidad." When the song ends the stage explodes in color. The*
8	*Christmas tree lights go on, with colored flashing lights, red chili*
9	*pepper lights, etc. The place is filled with color from top to bottom.*
10	*(All the GEMDALIANS "Oooo" and "Ahhh." Then they break*
11	*into applause. Everybody shouts out "Merry Christmas" to the*
12	*congregation in as many languages as possible, e.g. Feliz*
13	*Navidad, Frohe Weinachten, etc. Then the GEMDALIANS break*
14	*into "We Wish You a Merry Christmas.")*
15	*SONG:* "We Wish You a Merry Christmas."
16	**GEMDALIANS:** *(Singing)* **We wish you a merry Christmas,**
17	**We wish you a merry Christmas,**
18	**We wish you a merry Christmas,**
19	**And a happy new year!**
20	
21	**Good tidings we bring**
22	**To you and your kin,**
23	**Good tidings for Christmas**
24	**And a happy new year!**
25	
26	**We wish you a merry Christmas,**
27	**We wish you a merry Christmas,**
28	**We wish you a merry Christmas,**
29	**And a happy new year!**
30	
31	**Now bring us the figgy pudding,**
32	**Now bring us the figgy pudding,**
33	**Now bring us the figgy pudding,**
34	**And bring some right here!**
35	

1	We wish you a merry Christmas,
2	We wish you a merry Christmas,
3	We wish you a merry Christmas,
4	And a happy new year!
5	
6	For we all love our figgy pudding,
7	We all love our figgy pudding,
8	We all love our figgy pudding,
9	So bring some out here!
10	
11	And we won't go until we get some,
12	We won't go until we get some,
13	We won't go until we get some,
14	So bring some out here!
15	
16	We wish you a merry Chrstmas,
17	We wish you a merry Christmas,
18	We wish you a merry Christmas,
19	And a happy new year!
20	*(At the close of the song, the GEMDALIANS freeze and the lights*
21	*come down. Only the blazing tree is left in the darkness.)*
22	
23	
24	
25	
26	
27	
28	
29	
30	
31	
32	
33	
34	
35	

1   **SCENE ELEVEN**
2   "Grammieland"
3
4   *(The lights come up on GRAMMIE, JENNY and LISA.)*
5
6   **LISA: So that's a grand finale?**
7   **JENNY: That's right. And that's the end, too. Merry Christmas,**
8   **Lisa.**
9   **LISA: Merry Christmas, Jenny.**
10   **GRAMMIE:**   *(Eyes still closed)* **And Merry Christmas to both of**
11   **you.** *(She opens her eyes.)* **Now hit the hay, you two!** *(JENNY*
12   *and LISA run off laughing and shouting "Merry Christmas,*
13   *Grammie!" GRAMMIE watches them go. She smiles. Then she*
14   *looks around and goes to the radio. She switches it on. The lights*
15   *come up on the factory. The GEMDALIANS break into the*
16   *African-American gospel version of "Joy to the World!" They*
17   *move out into the congregation and down the aisles as they sing.)*
18
19
20
21
22
23
24
25
26
27
28
29
30
31
32
33
34
35

Red And Green

Enscoe, Hofer, Hopkins

Ornament Song

Enscoe, Hofer, McGowan

Glit - ter, glue some paint, too! All goes in the spark - ling stew to
make our tree bright or - na - ments that gleam and shine and make you "ooh!"
Bulbs and stars, an - gels fly, shapes you all must re - cog - nize, They shout: "Look!
Christ - mas is here!" To all the cheer - ful pass - ers by! What we hang on the tree is

THE TOWNE WITHOUT A TALE

A Medieval Christmas
Comedy
of
Pageant Proportions

L. G. Enscoe
Annie Enscoe

Larry Enscoe (L), Dean Batali, Cameron Carothers, Laura Hill and
Kevin King in a scene from the Glendale Presbyterian Church
production of *The Towne Without a Tale.*

150

THE TOWNE WITHOUT A TALE

CAST

NIGHT WATCHMAN

DUNLEY

VILLAGE MAYOR
(Your Minister)

VILLAGER ONE

VILLAGER TWO

VILLAGER THREE

OLD MAN WINTER

OLIVE

MIKE

DENNIS

BRIAN

THE MADRIGAL SINGERS

THE VILLAGE SINGERS
(All ages, from young to elderly)

THE MOON-AND-SUN PUPPETEER

FIVE SOLOISTS

WOMEN'S TRIO

PRODUCTION NOTES

Running Time

Seventy minutes.

Props

Padlock and chain (must be able to pull apart easily); sun and moon (one on each side — papier-mâché or stuffed cloth attached to pole); lantern; handbell; Dunley's scroll; Dunley's book (a large book made to look old); large baskets with vegetables, fruit, meat, cheeses, and breads inside; huge platter covered with holly (boar's head optional); giant, ancient map book; candles (enough for all the Madrigal Singers and Dunley); pile of laundry; goose (real or stuffed); cup; loaf of bread; crude hammer; sugar cubes; saw; small gifts.

Sound Effects

Crickets chirping; the ringing of Christmas bells; trumpet fanfare; flute trills. (All the sounds may be taped or you may have musicians provide the instrumental ones.)

Costumes

Medieval costumes again for the choirs and actors. The best route, if possible, is to rent them. We asked our singers and actors to come up with an occupation — a baker, a magistrate, a fruit seller, a monk, a tinsmith, a blacksmith, etc. — and then rent a costume that would display that. We also asked them to either carry or wear one prop that would make the occupation very clear to the audience.

If you decide not to rent, you can always make costumes. There are costume books in your local library that you can look to for inspiration. There are also some specialty patterns in fabric stores.

The four actors — Olive, Mike, Dennis and Brian — should be dressed like rustics in ratty, holey medieval clothes. When they play biblical characters, they should just slip on something traditional. Olive puts on a blue shawl. Brian puts on an overrobe and grabs a staff to play Joseph. Mike puts on an "oriental cap" — a turban or fez — to play the Innkeeper. We rented a stuffed donkey head for Dennis to use when he played the donkey. When Brian plays Scrooge, he just puts on a nightcap.

Putting on the biblical garb was done inside the wagon, or behind it, out of the view of the audience.

Dunley wears very rough peasant clothing. The Night Watchman wore a medieval constable's outfit. He also wore a modern sheriff's badge.

Old Man Winter is dressed in rags and wears a long, white beard. The "Boar's Head" soloist wears a butcher's apron and sports a festive holiday wreath on his/her head.

The troubador costume called for in the end of the play should be an outrageous bright doublet, stockings and a hat with a feather.

Set

We used an open platform sparsely set with benches, a hay wagon, hay bales, barrels, and a sign post to create the idea of a medieval village square. Fake snow bought in bags from either a floral supply or arts and crafts/hobby store can be applied liberally. We also used several dozen Christmas trees on the sides of the platforms to create a forest outside the village.

The risers for the choir (at Center Stage) were covered with a form-fitted tarp painted to look like stone. At the top of the riser or cathedral steps, we had two very large flats painted to look like giant cathedral doors. They were locked with a huge padlock and chains.

The pageant wagon was just a flatbed wagon large enough to hold three actors. We attached four spoked wooden wheels, raising it about four feet off the ground. There was a pull-handle hooked to the front so the actor could pull it On-stage (with the assistance of the other actors pushing from behind). We used a ladder so the actors could get on and off of it easily. Four posts about seven feet high were placed at the corners of the flatbed with rails connecting them. On the rails we hung bright fabric to make curtains. Patches adorned the curtains. You can attach the fabric to the rails like a shower curtain. The overall effect is like a four-poster bed.

Needless to say, the wagon was lumbering and could only be moved a dozen feet or so. We had it just Off-stage on a stage built off the sanctuary platform. Then we just rolled it straight onto the stage.

You can make the sun and moon out of papier-mâché — which you can buy in a hobby store — or out of fabric. We used fabric, stuffed and with a face sewn on. We made a quarter moon about three feet high, and the sun three feet in diameter. They were stuck on poles and held aloft by a person standing behind the cathedral doors. The poles being visible was part of the humor.

A crude wooden ramp leads up to the stage, Down Left. Holly and evergreen may be hung around.

SUGGESTED MUSIC SOURCES

"Past Three O'clock," G. R. Woodward, harmonized by Charles Wood, *Carols for Choirs 1*, Oxford University Press.

"Up Good Christian Fold and Listen!", G. R. Woodward, *Carols for Choirs 1*, Oxford University Press.

"The Holly and the Ivy," arr. John Rutter, Oxford University Press (and *Oxford Book of Carols*), Oxford University Press.

"The Wassail Song," *Oxford Book of Carols*.

"In the Bleak Midwinter," words by Christina Rosetti, music by Harold Dark, Galaxy Music.

"Rejoice and Be Merry," arr. Reginald Jacques, *Carols for Choirs 1*, Oxford University Press.

"Christ Is Born," (also known as "Il est ne le Divin Enfant"), French Traditional, arr. Marion Vree, Theodore Presser Company.

"The Angel Gabriel," adapt. by Carol P. Daw, Jr., *The Episcopal Hymnal 1982*, The Church Hymnal Corporation.

"Once in David's Royal City," C. F. Alexander and H. J. Gauntlett, harmonized by A. H. Mann, *Oxford Book of Carols*, Oxford University Press.

"Rocking," Czech carol, *Oxford Book of Carols*, Oxford University Press.

"The Boar's Head Carol," arr. Elizabeth Poston, *Carols for Choirs 1*, Oxford University Press.

"Deck the Halls," arr. Robert Shaw, Lawson-Gould Music Publishers, Inc.

"We Wish You a Merry Christmas," arr. Arthur Warrell, *Carols for Choirs 1*, Oxford University Press.

AUTHORS' NOTES

"The Christmas Story doesn't change, it changes us."

That's the concept behind this serious and comedic medieval Christmas pageant.

It follows the story of Dunley, a village poet and playwright, who hires a troupe of traveling actors to put on a Christmas pageant for his towne. When the actors change the story to "update it to the 1590s," Dunley steps in with the Villagers behind him to tell the real story.

This is a vivacious, theatrical and fast-moving romp of a pageant with a serious message about the power of the Gospel.

Most of the songs contained in this script were used in the original production. If you decide to use something of your own choice, or feel like you want to add more music, please feel free. Just take your theme cue from the lyrics included here and bring in your own material.

The Villagers should each decide on a character, then either make or rent a costume that fits it. There can also be one prop carried on in the first scene that says something about who they are in the towne society.

Keep light changes (if lights are available) and music cues sharp. This play really benefits from a quick pace.

The sun and the moon are worked by a backstage puppeteer hoisting them up on a pole. In our production, we made the sun and the moon actual characters by giving them a face and allowing them to react to what's going on On-stage by shaking, pulling back, and following the action.

Make the updated, "changed" pageant as theatrical and smarmy as possible. This way, the real Christmas story is made more powerful by its simplicity and joy.

SCENE ONE

(The play opens in a village square in winter. We hear the sound of crickets chirping. The lights come up in night colors. A figure is sleeping on the cathedral steps with a large book over his face. He is snoring. This is DUNLEY. He's a ragamuffin of a young man in his late teens or early twenties. The book is his bound notebook for writing down ideas. A bell tolls three times.

(DUNLEY hears the bells. He jumps up and quickly hides behind a barrel. The NIGHT WATCHMAN enters, carrying a lantern and tolling a handbell. He's dressed in a comic costume, vaguely like an officer's uniform. A tall, lanky actor would suit this character well.

(Oh, yes. It's the end of the Middle Ages. Christmas Eve morning. Friday. Three a.m.)

NIGHT WATCHMAN: **Three o'clock and all is well! Three o'clock and all is well! Three o'clock —** *(He stubs his toe in the dark and grabs his foot.)* **Three o'clock and my foot starts to swell!** *(The NIGHT WATCHMAN limps across the stage, tolling the bell.)* **Three *Ow*'clock! Three *Ouch*'clock! Three *Aah*'clock!**

(A SOLOIST steps into the moonlight. He or she is dressed in village clothes [or perhaps a street urchin, who offers a boy chorister opening]. A cappella, the SOLOIST begins singing. What will follow is a complete day in the village. Suggested song: "Past Three O'clock."

(The SOLOIST is joined by other voices Off-stage. At this time, there can be light musical accompaniment — a recorder, perhaps. The voices coming On-stage one by one to join the song will eventually create the MADRIGAL SINGERS, who will perform throughout the program. They walk on, dressed in the costumes of their trades, as they stretch and yawn, greeting one another sleepily. DUNLEY sneaks out to watch it all.

(Then bells ring. The lights begin to take on morning colors. A huge papier-mâché medieval sun begins moving above the stage,

1	*marking the time of day, as the moon moves off. The sprightly*
2	*accompaniment begins for "Up! Good Christian Folk and*
3	*Listen!" As the carol begins, the choir joins the MADRIGAL*
4	*SINGERS by twos and threes. They come out to greet the day.*
5	*The choir is, of course, the VILLAGERS, and all are dressed in*
6	*medieval garb.*
7	*(As we see them greeting the day, each one shows us his or her*
8	*character trait with costume, behavior and props: one lady is*
9	*carrying laundry; another man is carrying a goose; another is*
10	*begging, holding out a cup; another is a baker, holding a loaf*
11	*of bread; another is a woodsmith, holding a crude hammer;*
12	*another is selling vegetables; and so on. A gradual swelling of*
13	*people On-stage.*
14	*(During the song, DUNLEY goes to VILLAGERS, tapping them*
15	*on the shoulders and throwing open a book as if to read them a*
16	*story. All shake their heads and wave him away.)*
17	**SONG:** "Up! Good Christian Folk and Listen!"
18	**VILLAGERS AND MADRIGAL SINGERS:** *(Singing)* **Ding-**
19	**dong, ding: ding-a-dong-a-ding,**
20	**Ding-dong, ding: ding-a-dong-a-ding.**
21	
22	**Ding-dong, ding: ding-a-dong-a-ding,**
23	**Ding-dong, ding: ding-a-dong-a-ding.**
24	
25	**Up good Christian folk and listen**
26	**How the merry church bells ring.**
27	**And from steeple, bid good people**
28	**Come adore the newborn King.**
29	
30	**Ding-dong, ding: ding-a-dong-a-ding,**
31	**Ding-dong, ding: ding-a-dong-a-ding.**
32	
33	**Tell the story, how from glory**
34	**God came down at Christmastide,**
35	**Bringing gladness, chasing sadness**

1   **Show'ring blessings far and wide.**
2

3   **Ding-dong, ding: ding-a-dong-a-ding**
4   **Ding-dong, ding: ding-a-dong-a-ding.**
5

6   **Born of mother, blest o'er other,**
7   **Ex Maria Virgine,**
8   **In a stable, 'tis no fable**
9   **Christus natus hodie.**
10

11   **Ding-dong, ding: ding-a-dong-a-ding**
12   **Ding-dong, ding: ding-a-dong-a-ding.**
13

14   **Ding-dong, ding: ding-a-dong-a-ding**
15   **Ding-dong, ding: ding-a-dong-a-ding.**
16   *(By the end of the carol, the lights have become very bright. It's*
17   *now afternoon. The sun on its pole is straight up over the*
18   *padlocked cathedral doors. All the VILLAGERS and*
19   *MADRIGAL SINGERS should be on stage now, greeting one*
20   *another and laughing, selling, showing their wares, playing*
21   *games, and going on with the festive business of the day in a*
22   *small medieval village on the verge of Christmas.*
23   *(The music begins for "The Holly and the Ivy." Someone comes*
24   *through with baskets of holly sprigs. They hand them out to the*
25   *VILLAGERS and MADRIGAL SINGERS. A SOLOIST or*
26   *SOLOISTS begins the carol, with the VILLAGERS and*
27   *MADRIGAL SINGERS taking the chorus.)*
28 *SONG:*   "The Holly and the Ivy."
29 **SOLOIST:** *(Singing)* **The holly and the ivy,**
30   **When they are both full grown,**
31   **Of all the trees that are in the wood,**
32   **The holly tree bears the crown.**
33

34 *CHORUS:* *(VILLAGERS/MADRIGAL SINGERS)* **The rising**
35   **of the sun,**

1	And the running of the deer,
2	The playing of the merry organ,
3	Sweet singing in the choir.
4	
5	*(SOLOIST)* The holly bears a blossom
6	As white as the lily flower,
7	And Mary bore sweet Jesus Christ,
8	To be our sweet Saviour.
9	
10	*CHORUS: (VILLAGERS/MADRIGAL SINGERS)*
11	
12	*(SOLOIST)* The holly bears a berry,
13	As red as any blood,
14	And Mary bore sweet Jesus Christ
15	To do poor sinners good.
16	
17	*CHORUS: (VILLAGERS/MADRIGAL SINGERS)*
18	
19	*(SOLOIST)* The holly bears a prickle
20	As sharp as any thorn,
21	And Mary bore sweet Jesus Christ,
22	On Christmas Day in the morn.
23	
24	*CHORUS: (VILLAGERS/MADRIGAL SINGERS)*
25	*(At the close of the carol, the VILLAGE MAYOR [played by your*
26	*minister] steps forward to greet the audience.)*
27	**VILLAGE MAYOR:** I welcome you all to our village square
28	Where you'll find hints of Christmas —
29	Some here and some there.
30	A holly sprig with red berry,
31	A bough of evergreen.
32	All bright reminders of the coming
33	Christmas e'en.
34	
35	Tarry with us, warm your hearts by our fire.

1   **Listen to the voices of our well-rehearsed choir.**
2   **So, the music is learned and the stage has been set.**
3   **I promise thee, good folk . . . you ain't seen nothin' yet!**
4   **VILLAGER ONE: Tell us the Christmas story, Mayor!** *(The*
5   *VILLAGE MAYOR looks back at the cathedral doors. He walks*
6   *up to them, patting the padlock.)*
7   **VILLAGE MAYOR: Good villagers, I wish I could tell the**
8   **story. But as you all know, I'm no parson. We must wait**
9   **till God sees fit to fill our pulpit again.** *(The VILLAGERS*
10   *groan. DUNLEY jumps onto the cathedral steps, throwing open*
11   *his book. A bright light hits him with a trill.)*
12   **DUNLEY:**   *(Brightly)* **Villagers all! Let us wait no longer! I can**
13   **tell the story! I have composed a Christmas pageant for**
14   **the whole town!** *(The VILLAGERS turn and stare at him.)*
15   **VILLAGER ONE: Aw, that's just Dunley, the village poet!**
16   **VILLAGER TWO: Bohemian!**
17   **VILLAGER THREE: Yeah, get a job!** *(Then the VILLAGERS*
18   *break out laughing. DUNLEY hangs his head, closing the book.*
19   *The VILLAGERS turn to each other with "Merry Christmases."*
20   *The sun moves toward evening. The lights begin to take on night*
21   *colors. The music begins for "Here We Come A-Wassailing."*
22   *During the song, the VILLAGERS begin to move off the stage.*
23   *They leave by twos and threes just as they came on. [They deposit*
24   *their holly sprigs Off-stage during this.] They leave the*
25   *MADRIGAL SINGERS and SOLOIST On-stage.)*
26   *SONG:*   "Here We Come A-Wassailing."
27   **MADRIGAL SINGERS:**   *(Singing)* **Here we come a-wassailing**
28   **Among the leaves so green,**
29   **Here we come a-wand'ring**
30   **So fair to be seen.**
31
32   **Love and joy come to you,**
33   **And to you, your wassail too,**
34   **And God bless you and send you**
35   **A happy new year,**

161

1	And God send you a happy new year.
2	
3	We are not daily beggars
4	That be from door to door,
5	We are your neighbor's children,
6	Whom you have seen before.
7	
8	Love and joy come to you,
9	And to you, your wassail too,
10	And God bless you and send you
11	A happy new year,
12	And God send you a happy new year.
13	
14	God bless the master of this house,
15	Likewise, the mistress too,
16	And all the little children
17	That round the table go.
18	
19	Love and joy come to you,
20	And to you, your wassail too,
21	And God bless you and send you
22	A happy new year,
23	And God send you a happy new year.
24	*(At the final chorus, the VILLAGERS' voices are very soft, as if*
25	*far away. As people go, DUNLEY tries to get their attention.*
26	*Everyone rushes off, ignoring him. The stage takes on night*
27	*colors. The sun falls asleep in the west. DUNLEY sits down,*
28	*reading from his book, smiling or laughing to himself and*
29	*sighing at the touching parts. The MADRIGAL SINGERS are*
30	*left On-stage to sing. Suggested song: "Past Three O'clock." As*
31	*the song nears its end, the MADRIGAL SINGERS leave the*
32	*stage one by one, yawning and stretching and bidding good night*
33	*to one another, until finally only the SOLOIST is left. The*
34	*SOLOIST who began the scene sings the final chorus.*
35	*(The NIGHT WATCHMAN walks through, ringing his bell.)*

1   **NIGHT WATCHMAN: Three o'clock and all is well! Three**
2   **o'clock and all is well!** *(The SOLOIST, if a street urchin*
3   *concept is used, can sneak past the NIGHT WATCHMAN,*
4   *stealing something out of his pocket and running off. The NIGHT*
5   *WATCHMAN chases after him as the lights go to blackout.)*
6
7
8
9
10
11
12
13
14
15
16
17
18
19
20
21
22
23
24
25
26
27
28
29
30
31
32
33
34
35

1	**SCENE TWO**
2	
3	*(The sound of crickets fills the air. In the darkness, there is*
4	*movement. It sounds like creaky wooden wheels. Then we hear*
5	*the sound of someone straining, as if she is lifting something*
6	*heavy. Then the moon pops up over the cathedral doors.*
7	*Moonlight floods the stage. We are looking at a large pageant*
8	*wagon. The wagon is positioned directly in front of the cathedral*
9	*doors, and it's being pulled by a weary wisp of a young woman.*
10	*Her name is OLIVE.)*
11	**OLIVE: That's it. I'm done. We're stopping here for the night.**
12	*(A beat. The pageant wagon curtains part and three faces peek*
13	*out. They are MIKE, DENNIS and BRIAN. Along with OLIVE,*
14	*they are the ACTORS.)*
15	**MIKE: We're here!** *(Looks around.)* **Where are we?**
16	**OLIVE: I have no idea, but I'm not pulling this thing**
17	**anymore. Everybody out.** *(MIKE, DENNIS and BRIAN*
18	*tumble out of the wagon. They stretch and yawn. BRIAN is*
19	*looking at a giant ancient map book.)*
20	**DENNIS: Aw, we're in the middle of nowhere, that's where**
21	**we are.**
22	**BRIAN: Friends, I hate to tell you this, but this place isn't on**
23	**the Double A map.**
24	**MIKE:** *(Snatching the map book away)* **Give me that.** *(He looks at*
25	*it.)* **You're right.** *(Slams the book closed.)* **I can hardly wait**
26	**till they update this thing to a Triple A map.**
27	**DENNIS: I say let's push on till we find a place that gets us**
28	**on the map.**
29	**OLIVE: Forget it. I am *not* pulling that wagon any farther**
30	**tonight. I don't know why we can't get a horse.**
31	**MIKE: Do you know what the overhead on a horse would be?**
32	**You only eat half as much as a real horse.** *(OLIVE grabs*
33	*him by the ear.)* **Oh, come on, we stopped makin' you wear**
34	**the bridle, didn't we?** *(He pulls sugar cubes out of his pocket*
35	*and "nicks" to her, beckoning her.)* **Here, have some sugar.**

1 *(OLIVE elbows him. The NIGHT WATCHMAN tolls his bell*
2 *from Off-stage.)*
3 **NIGHT WATCHMAN:** *(Off-stage)* **Three twenty-nine and**
4 **thirty seconds!** *(OLIVE, MIKE, DENNIS and BRIAN*
5 *scramble into the wagon. The NIGHT WATCHMAN is coming*
6 *up the aisle.)* **Three twenty-nine and forty seconds! Three**
7 **twenty-nine and fifty seconds.** *(Lifts the bell high. In a*
8 *telephone operator voice)* **At the tone, the time will be three-**
9 **thirty a.m. Exactly.** *(He sounds the bell. Then he notices the*
10 *wagon sitting there.)* **Ho, there. What is this? Halt. I mean,**
11 **who goes there?** *(Silence from within the wagon.)* ***Show***
12 ***yourselves!*** *(Suddenly the curtain is thrown open, and OLIVE,*
13 *MIKE, DENNIS and BRIAN are in an outrageously melodra-*
14 *matic tableau. The NIGHT WATCHMAN looks at the audience.)*
15 **Great. Actors.**
16 **MIKE:** No, sir, you mean great actors!
17 **DENNIS:** And more, good sir!
18 **OLIVE:** We're tragedians!
19 **BRIAN:** Thespians!
20 **MIKE:** Harlequins!
21 **OLIVE:** Mummers!
22 **DENNIS:** Melodramitians!
23 **OLIVE:** Monologists!
24 **MIKE:** Pantomimists!
25 **BRIAN:** Antagonists!
26 **MIKE:** Protagonists!
27 **NIGHT WATCHMAN:** **Obnoxious!** *(They all stare at him in*
28 *various poses of hurt, shock, outrage, etc. The NIGHT*
29 *WATCHMAN waves them on.)* **You'll have to get that wagon**
30 **out of here.** *(The ACTORS tumble out of the wagon. MIKE*
31 *immediately goes into an act.)*
32 **MIKE:** But why, sir? We have traveled over miles and miles
33 of bumpy, dusty, dangerous road just to bring joy to this
34 very village.
35 **NIGHT WATCHMAN:** This, you knaves, is the town of

1   _____. *(Make up medieval town based on your city.)*

2   **MIKE: Of course, it's the town of** _____**! The very**

3   **grail of our long, long journey!**

4   **NIGHT WATCHMAN: Well, since you've traveled so far, I'm**

5   **sure you won't mind a few more feet. Now move that**

6   **wagon!**

7   **OLIVE: *(Flirty)* But, good sir, this is where we shall play our**

8   **play!**

9   **NIGHT WATCHMAN: Not in front of the cathedral, you don't.**

10   *(The ACTORS swing a look at the huge cathedral doors behind*

11   *them.)*

12   **DENNIS: Forsooth, why? Are you telling us that actors are**

13   **not *welcome* here on holy church ground?!**

14   **NIGHT WATCHMAN: Heck no. You're parked in the white**

15   **zone. *(To the audience)* The white zone is for loading and**

16   **unloading only. No exceptions. *(To the ACTORS)* Now**

17   **move that vehicle before I impound it. *(The NIGHT***

18   *WATCHMAN starts to go.)*

19   **OLIVE: Wait, good sir! Why, pray you, are the cathedral doors**

20   **locked? Should the church doors not be open to everyone**

21   **who desires to draw nigh? *(The ACTORS murmur in***

22   *agreement.)*

23   **NIGHT WATCHMAN: Alas . . . the church doors are locked**

24   **because . . . because . . . *(He begins to weep)* . . . because we**

25   **have no parson! *(The NIGHT WATCHMAN sits on a stump,***

26   *sobbing. The ACTORS see a weakness and immediately dash*

27   *over to him to exploit it.)*

28   **DENNIS: Oh . . . forsooth, how long have you been deprived**

29   **of a man of the cloth?**

30   **NIGHT WATCHMAN: Forsooth, since the late 1400s.**

31   **MIKE: Forsooth, that is a tale of great woe, sir.**

32   **OLIVE: Forsooth, why are we all talking like this?**

33   **NIGHT WATCHMAN: I don't know, you guys started it.**

34   **MIKE: Please go on with your sad story, Monsieur Watchman.**

35   **NIGHT WATCHMAN: *(Begins sobbing again.)* It's not that we**

1   **didn't try to find someone to fill our pulpit. The Parson**
2   **Search Committee started looking for a candidate a few**
3   **years after the Black Plague. What is it now . . . ?** *(Looks*
4   *at his watch and whistles.)* **Almost the Rensaissance.**
5   **BRIAN:**   **That's a long search, indeed.**
6   **NIGHT WATCHMAN:**   **Well, we're particular.** *(Suddenly OLD*
7   *MAN WINTER enters [or use name of the real person]. He's*
8   *talking to himself, trying to catch flies, giggling and twitching.*
9   *In other words . . . he's crazy.)*
10   **DENNIS:**   **Who is that?**
11   **OLIVE:**   **Poor soul.**
12   **NIGHT WATCHMAN:**   **That's Old Man Winter. He headed the**
13   **Parson Search Committee for sixty years. Finally drove**
14   **him mad.** *(OLD MAD WINTER twitches past them all and*
15   *exits.)* **Well, now, you Harlequins better have that wagon**
16   **moved by the time I get back!** *(The NIGHT WATCHMAN*
17   *walks off, tolling the bell.)* **Four o'clock and all is well! Four**
18   **o'clock and all is well!** *(The ACTORS watch him go. MIKE,*
19   *DENNIS and BRIAN look at each other, then make a dash for*
20   *the wagon. They jump inside and pull the curtain closed in*
21   *OLIVE's face. OLIVE stomps toward the wagon hitch and picks*
22   *it up.)*
23   **OLIVE:**   **Look! This is *not* in my contract!** *(Blackout)*
24
25
26
27
28
29
30
31
32
33
34
35

1	<div align="center">**SCENE THREE**</div>
2	
3	*(Darkness. The MADRIGAL SINGERS come in carrying*
4	*candles. The wagon is no longer On-stage. The MADRIGAL*
5	*SINGERS begin "In the Bleak Midwinter.")*
6	***SONG:*** "In the Bleak Midwinter."
7	**MADRIGAL SINGERS:** *(Singing)* **In the bleak midwinter,**
8	**Frosty wind made moan.**
9	**Earth stood hard as iron,**
10	**Water like a stone.**
11	
12	**Snow had fallen, snow on snow,**
13	**Snow on snow,**
14	**In the bleak midwinter**
15	**Long ago.**
16	
17	**Our God, heaven cannot hold him,**
18	**Nor earth sustain;**
19	**Heav'n and earth shall welcome him**
20	**When he comes to reign:**
21	
22	**In the bleak midwinter,**
23	**A stable place sufficed.**
24	**The Lord God incarnate,**
25	**Jesus Christ.**
26	
27	**What can I give him, poor as I am?**
28	**If I were a shepherd,**
29	**I would bring a lamb;**
30	**If I were a wise man,**
31	**I would do my part;**
32	**Yet what I can, I give him:**
33	**Give my heart.**
34	*(The MADRIGAL SINGERS blow out their candles. The stage*
35	*goes to blackout.)*

SCENE FOUR

(Dawn's early light comes up. The sun has barely risen. The NIGHT WATCHMAN can be heard in the distance ringing his handbell.)

NIGHT WATCHMAN: Five o'clock and all is well! Five o'clock and all is well! *(DUNLEY pops up from behind the barrel, holding a candle. He slips across the stage and down into the trees, left. He reaches the wagon. It's parked off to the side. We can hear the snoring of the ACTORS inside.)*

DUNLEY: Pssst. *(Nothing from inside the wagon. Just the snoring. DUNLEY sneaks a little closer. Whispers.)* Hey. Hey, inside. **Thespians. Tragedians. Comedians.** *(Still nothing)* **I want to hire you.** *(The snoring stops. The curtains are thrown back and the ACTORS jump out.)*

MIKE: We get ten percent of the box office up front, plus we get an option that gives us a back-end deal. And we each get our own separate wagons.

DUNLEY: What? *(The ACTORS look closely at him.)*

OLIVE: C'mon, he's just a ragamuffin. *(The ACTORS start to get back into the wagon.)*

DUNLEY: *(Holds out his book.)* But wait, I've written a play.

DENNIS: You and everybody's mother.

BRIAN: Now be off with you.

DUNLEY: No, wait! I — I've written a Christmas play. Sort of a . . . pageant. Gosh, we haven't had a parson in here in years, so nobody's heard the Christmas story. There's been no one to tell it. I mean, nobody's been to church in years around here, so I thought we could bring the Christmas story out to them on Christmas day. *(On cue, the Christmas bells start ringing. The ACTORS look toward the village. BRIAN jumps up into the wagon and pulls on a droopy nightcap. He speaks in a creaky old voice.)*

BRIAN: What's today?

DUNLEY: Eh?

1   BRIAN: What's today, my fine fellow?

2   DUNLEY: Today? Why, it's Christmas Day! *(BRIAN starts*
3   *jumping around, grabbing the curtains like bed curtains.)*

4   BRIAN: Then I haven't missed it! The Spirits of Christmas
5   Past, Present and Future. They have done it all in one
6   night! They can do anything they like. Of course they
7   can! Of course they can! *(BRIAN notices everyone staring at*
8   *him.)* Sorry. It's this idea for a script I've been working
9   on. See, it's about this evil, grasping old sinner named
10   Scrooge —

11   MIKE: No one will buy it. *(BRIAN drops his head, wounded.*
12   *MIKE turns to DUNLEY.)* Do you have your Christmas
13   pageant with you, dear boy?

14   DUNLEY: *(Pulling a script out of the book)* I should hope I do.

15   BRIAN: *(Scrooge voice)* An intelligent boy. A remarkable boy!
16   *(Everyone gives him a look.)* Sorry.

17   MIKE: *(Looking the script over)* Friends, I have an idea. We shall
18   give _____ *(Town name here)* its very own
19   Christmas pageant!

20   OLIVE: Is there a part in it for me?

21   MIKE: An innocent young maiden? I don't know. *(She grabs*
22   *his ear.)* Maybe we can work you in.

23   DENNIS: Now look here! I'm not playing any animals this
24   time. That aardvark suit in Newcastle last year was the
25   last straw.

26   BRIAN: *(Leaping from the wagon)* No! We'll use real barn
27   animals. *Live* animals. Yes, live animals coming down the
28   aisles. Sheep, donkeys, camels, pigs! And we'll have
29   angels. Lots of angels. *(BRIAN grabs OLIVE and starts*
30   *swinging her.)* Yes, we'll fly them in overhead on wires.
31   We'll have angels flying over the audience's heads! *(He*
32   *lets OLIVE loose. She goes sailing off.)*

33   MIKE: Do you know what kind of budget we'd need for flying
34   angels?

35   BRIAN: Well . . .

1   **DENNIS:** Besides, that's a little over the top, don't you
2   **think?**
3   **OLIVE:** Next he's gonna want a cast of thousands.
4   **MIKE:** It's crystal clear to me.
5   **BRIAN:** OK, forget the flying angels! Maybe we could just
6   **have *one* angel hanging from a tree . . . ?**
7   **ALL ACTORS:** Uh-uh.
8   **BRIAN:** OK, how about a live pig? *(The other ACTORS glare at*
9   *him.)*
10   **DUNLEY:** Will you do my play?
11   **MIKE:** We shall, good lad! This day _____ *(Town*
12   *name here)* **will have its very own Christmas pageant —**
13   **one like it's never seen before!** *(He takes the book.)* **Of**
14   **course, we get all rights in perpetuity, and the play**
15   **becomes the intellectual property of Medieval Village**
16   **Pageants, Incorporated.** *(DUNLEY looks at the audience. He*
17   *has no idea what they're talking about.)*
18   **BRIAN:** *(Pointing at DENNIS)* **Why can't we dress him up like**
19   **a pig?**
20   **DENNIS:** Forget it! *(OLIVE jumps between DENNIS and BRIAN*
21   *as the lights go to blackout.)*
22
23
24
25
26
27
28
29
30
31
32
33
34
35

1   **SCENE FIVE**

2

3   *(The Christmas bells peal loudly. The lights come up bright. The*

4   *medieval sun marks its way over the village sky. The*

5   *VILLAGERS come in, singing "Rejoice and Be Merry" a*

6   *cappella. They greet each other with hugs, handshakes and small*

7   *gifts. DUNLEY is watching it all from behind his barrel. He's*

8   *grinning like a canary-eating cat.)*

9   **SONG:**   "Rejoice and Be Merry."

10   **VILLAGERS:**   *(Singing)* **Rejoice and be merry in songs and in**

11   **mirth!**

12   **O praise our Redeemer, all mortals on earth!**

13   **For this is the birthday of Jesus our King,**

14   **Who brought us salvation — his praises we'll sing!**

15

16   **A heavenly vision appeared in the sky;**

17   **Vast numbers of angels the shepherds did spy,**

18   **Proclaiming the birthday of Jesus our King,**

19   **Who brought us salvation — his praises we'll sing!**

20

21   **Likewise a bright star in the sky did appear,**

22   **Which led the wise men from the east to draw near;**

23   **They found the Messiah, sweet Jesus our King,**

24   **Who brought us salvation — his praises we'll sing!**

25

26   **And when they were come, they their treasures unfold,**

27   **And unto him offered myrrh, incense and gold,**

28   **So blessed forever be Jesus our King,**

29   **Who brought us salvation — his praises we'll sing!**

30   *(The music begins for "Christ Is Born." A WOMEN'S TRIO*

31   *comes forward as the VILLAGERS sit on the stone steps, hay*

32   *bales, benches, and stumps to listen.)*

33   **SONG:**   "Christ Is Born."

34   **WOMEN'S TRIO:**   *(Singing)* **Christ is born, the holy Child,**

35   **Play the musette, the tuneful oboe;**

1	He is born, the holy Child,
2	Christ the Lord is born today.
3	
4	On a manger bed he lay,
5	In a stable, cold and bare;
6	On a manger bed he lay,
7	Kneel before the Child today.
8	*CHORUS:* Ah, what beauty to behold!
9	See him there, the divine Christ child.
10	Ah, what beauty to behold!
11	Glows so softly with light divine.
12	*(Repeat chorus.)*
13	*(Suddenly there's a trumpet fanfare. The VILLAGERS look*
14	*around in surprise. The lights come up on the pageant wagon.*
15	*The patched curtains are thrown open, and MIKE, in a bad*
16	*biblical costume, steps down to greet them.)*
17	**MIKE:** **Ladies and gentlemen! We welcome you this Christmas**
18	**day to our small seasonal offering.** *(DUNLEY pops up from*
19	*behind his barrel and applauds. The VILLAGERS just stare at*
20	*him. DUNLEY winces and sits.)* **We hope you will enjoy the**
21	**fruits of our weeks of hard labor. And now, folks,**
22	**peasants, large landowners and all, we bring you . . .**
23	*(Ominously)* **"The Dark Streets of Bethlehem."** *(The*
24	*VILLAGERS babble to each other in dismay. DUNLEY looks*
25	*at the audience.)*
26	**DUNLEY:** **"The Dark Streets of Bethlehem"? But *my* play's**
27	**called "The Littlest Manger."** *(MIKE pulls open the curtains.*
28	*The ACTORS are arguing. OLIVE and BRIAN are dressed like*
29	*Mary and Joseph. DENNIS is wearing a donkey head, and he's*
30	*not happy about it. They see the audience and immediately get*
31	*into position. OLIVE sits on DENNIS's back. BRIAN stands*
32	*nearby. They start making wind sounds.)*
33	**MIKE:** **It was a dark and stormy night in Bethlehem. A night**
34	**not fit for man nor beast.** *(DENNIS brays — not happily.)*
35	**The frozen streets were crammed with the castoff odds**

173

1 **and ends of humanity. Into this dark and dangerous pit**
2 **of overcrowded urban sprawl, they came. Mary and**
3 **Joseph. Young, sweet, naive. Though they had been the**
4 **focus of a scandal that had rocked the nation only months**
5 **before.** *(The VILLAGERS look confused by this revised version.*
6 *They whisper their surprise and dismay. DUNLEY is beside*
7 *himself.)*
8 DUNLEY: Wait a minute . . .
9 MIKE: *(Ignoring DUNLEY)* **Mary was great with child. Joseph**
10 **was great with a saw. And he was willing to do anything**
11 **to get them a room for the night. Anything.** *(MIKE sticks*
12 *on an Oriental cap and stands in front of OLIVE and BRIAN,*
13 *barring the way. MIKE is now the INNKEEPER.)* **Didn't ya**
14 **hear me the first time, buddy? I said, no room.**
15 BRIAN: **But please, sir . . . my wife is with child —**
16 MIKE: **Not my problem, pal. Now hit the road.**
17 BRIAN: *(Imitating Clint Eastwood)* **You crossed the wrong guy,**
18 **fella.** *(We hear the famous flute trill from* The Good, The Bad
19 and the Ugly.*)*
20 MIKE: **Yeah?**
21 BRIAN: **Yeah. Let us in, or I'll saw your inn down.** *(BRIAN*
22 *whips out a saw. MIKE throws up his hands. The VILLAGERS*
23 *gasp. DUNLEY can't take it anymore.)*
24 DUNLEY: **Wait a minute! This isn't the play I wrote. This isn't**
25 **the Christmas story. What is this?**
26 MIKE: **Give us a break, kid. We're trying to work up here.**
27 DUNLEY: **That's not the Christmas pageant I wrote.**
28 MIKE: **Well, your story was a little soft, kid. We needed to**
29 **inject a little drama into it. Give it a little** *edge.*
30 DUNLEY: **Drama? God coming to earth as a baby? Angels**
31 **appearing in the sky? Astronomical wonders? That's not**
32 **drama?**
33 OLIVE: **C'mon, these folks've heard that ol' story a hundred**
34 **times. We need to change things a little. You know . . .**
35 **bring it into the 1590s.**

174

1   **BRIAN:**   You tell the same story too many times, you lose your
2   **audience.**
3   **DUNLEY:**   But this is a story that can't be told too many times.
4   *(He gets up on the wagon ladder and turns to the VILLAGERS.*
5   *He looks for all the world like a preacher.)* **Villagers! Don't**
6   **you see?! The Christmas story doesn't change. It changes**
7   **us.** *(The VILLAGERS murmur their agreement.)*
8   **MIKE:**   Who's telling this tale, kid — you or us? *(A beat.*
9   *DUNLEY looks at the VILLAGERS. He grins.)*
10   **DUNLEY:**   Us . . . ? *(The VILLAGERS are with him.)*
11   **VILLAGERS:**   *Us!* *(DUNLEY beams. The VILLAGERS cheer.*
12   *The ACTORS pout.)*
13   **MIKE:**   Well, that's just fine!
14   **OLIVE:**   Tell it yourselves!
15   **DENNIS:**   No skin off our mistletoe!
16   **BRIAN:**   *(Imitating Clint Eastwood)* **But you just missed the best**
17   **little pageant ever.** *(BRIAN raises the saw like a gun. The*
18   *famous flute trill is heard again. Blackout.)*
19
20
21
22
23
24
25
26
27
28
29
30
31
32
33
34
35

1 **SCENE SIX**
2
3   *(The lights come up on a MALE SOLOIST. He sings verses one*
4   *and two of "The Angel Gabriel." The third verse is sung by the*
5   *FEMALE SOLOIST, the fourth by the VILLAGERS.)*
6   *SONG:* "The Angel Gabriel." *(Verses one and two)*
7   **MALE SOLOIST:** *(Singing)* **The angel Gabriel from heaven**
8   **came,**
9   **His wings as drifted snow, his eyes as flame,**
10 **"All hail," said he, "thou lowly maiden Mary,**
11 **Most highly favored lady," Gloria!**
12
13 **"For know a blessed mother shalt thou be,**
14 **All generations laud and honor thee,**
15 **Thy Son shall be Emmanuel, by seers foretold,**
16 **Most highly favored lady," Gloria!**
17 *(The carol music continues softly. The VILLAGERS part to reveal*
18 *DUNLEY standing in front of the cathedral doors.)*
19 **DUNLEY:** **Our play begins like this . . .** *(DUNLEY looks over at*
20 *the wagon. He sees the ACTORS have popped their faces out.*
21 *When they see him looking, they pull back inside.)* **God sent**
22 **the angel Gabriel to Galilee to a small town called**
23 **Nazareth to a young woman engaged to a carpenter**
24 **named Joseph. The young woman's name was . . .**
25 *(Suddenly, the curtains on the wagon part. OLIVE is looking at*
26 *him.)* **The young woman's name was Mary.** *(OLIVE nods.*
27 *She steps down out of the wagon dressed as Mary. She walks*
28 *toward the village square. The other ACTORS, particularly*
29 *MIKE, try to stop her. The VILLAGERS gasp and whisper.*
30 *DUNLEY smiles at OLIVE. He walks toward her. He takes her*
31 *hand.)* **And the angel said, "Hail, Mary, full of grace,**
32 **blessed are you among women."**
33 **OLIVE:** **Mary was terrified, but the angel said:** *(DENNIS is*
34 *suddenly standing on the wagon steps.)*
35 **DENNIS:** **Don't be afraid, Mary!** *(MIKE taps DENNIS on the*

176

1   *shoulder. DENNIS ignores him and steps down.)*

2   **DUNLEY:**   Mary was surprised to see the angel Gabriel. The

3   angel continued his message.

4   **DENNIS:** *(Walking toward them)* **I have come to bring you good**

5   news. Very soon now, you will be with child. You will

6   give birth to a son. And you will give him the name Jesus.

7   **OLIVE:**   How can this be? I have not been with a man.

8   **DENNIS:**   The power of God will overshadow you. The child

9   born will be called ... the Son of God. *(The FEMALE*

10   *SOLOIST begins to sing the third verse of "The Angel Gabriel,"*

11   *followed by the VILLAGERS on the fourth.)*

12   *SONG:* "The Angel Gabriel." *(Verses three and four)*

13   **FEMALE SOLOIST:**   Then gentle Mary meekly bowed her head,

14   "To me be as it pleaseth God," she said,

15   "My soul shall laud and magnify his holy Name."

16   Most highly favored lady, Gloria!

17   **VILLAGERS:**   Of her, Emmanuel, the Christ was born

18   In Bethlehem, all on a Christmas morn,

19   And Christian folk throughout the world will ever say,

20   "Most highly favored lady," Gloria.

21   **DUNLEY:**   But the first person to hear the news of the Son of

22   God was a carpenter shaking sawdust out of his hair.

23   *(DUNLEY looks toward the wagon.)* **The carpenter's name**

24   was Joseph. *(We can see a scuffle behind the curtain. BRIAN*

25   *steps out of the wagon. He looks back at MIKE, glaring at him.*

26   *He walks toward OLIVE.)* **Joseph did not believe a word of**

27   what he was told. Fear, anger, and pain stood in the way

28   of his believing. The things that have always stood in the

29   way.

30   We might not all find angels at our bedside telling

31   us the truth, but Joseph did. Perhaps that's what it took.

32   But Joseph did believe. And that belief found Joseph and

33   Mary trudging into Bethlehem in the middle of the night,

34   birth-ready and nowhere near a decent place to bring

35   Jesus into the world. But decent or not, Jesus was coming.

1	*(As the MADRIGAL SINGERS sing "Once in Royal David's*
2	*City," BRIAN takes OLIVE's arm and leads her through the*
3	*VILLAGERS, who turn their faces from them. They are MARY*
4	*and JOSEPH looking for a room. They even knock at the closed*
5	*and locked cathedral doors.)*
6	***SONG:*** "Once in Royal David's City."
7	**MADRIGAL SINGERS:** *(Singing)* **Once in royal David's city**
8	**Stood a lowly cattle shed,**
9	**Where a mother laid her baby**
10	**In a manger for his bed:**
11	**Mary was that mother mild,**
12	**Jesus Christ her little child.**
13	
14	**He came down to earth from heaven**
15	**Who is God and Lord of all,**
16	**And his shelter was a stable,**
17	**And his cradle was a stall;**
18	**With the poor and mean and lowly**
19	**Lived on earth, our Savior holy.**
20	
21	**Not in that poor lowly stable,**
22	**With the oxen standing by,**
23	**We shall see him; but in heaven,**
24	**Set at God's right hand on high;**
25	**Where like stars his children crowned**
26	**All in white, shall wait around.**
27	*(OLIVE and BRIAN finally arrive at the wagon.)*
28	**DUNLEY:** And while they were in Bethlehem, the time came
29	for the child to be born. *(BRIAN knocks on the wagon. Silence.*
30	*He knocks on the wagon again. Silence. He goes to knock . . .*
31	*MIKE pops his head out. He looks like he's about to chew their*
32	*heads off. MIKE sees the audience staring at him. He can't resist*
33	*an audience. He rolls his eyes and pops back inside the wagon.*
34	*A beat. MIKE throws back the curtains. He's wearing the*
35	*Innkeeper's cap.)*

178

1   **MIKE:**   Go on, you two. You heard me, no room. Full up. Up
2   to here. Move on. Keep moving. Nothing to see here.
3   **BRIAN:**   Please, sir. Any room will do.
4   **MIKE:**   *Any* room? Well ... *(He grins)* ... I've got this scary,
5   dark castle out back you can stay in. *(He turns to the*
6   *audience.)* **And so Mary and Joseph made their way across**
7   **a moat filled with giant, Bible-character-eating crocodiles,**
8   **and then they both climbed this thorn-covered wall —**
9   *(OLIVE tugs on MIKE's cuff. She gives him a look.)* **OK, I've**
10   **got a boring old stable you can stay in. It's not much, but**
11   **you're welcome to it.** *(MIKE yanks the curtains closed. BRIAN*
12   *leads OLIVE round back of the wagon.)*
13   **DUNLEY:**   **Mary gave birth to her first-born. And Joseph**
14   **gave him the name Jesus.** *(A SOLOIST comes forward and*
15   *sings a song about the birth of Christ. [The original production*
16   *used "Joseph's Song" by Michael Card and sung by DUNLEY.]*
17   *At the close of the solo, DUNLEY goes to the wagon. He sighs and*
18   *pulls open the curtains. OLIVE and BRIAN are in a traditional*
19   *tender crèche scene. The floor of the wagon is strewn with hay. OLIVE*
20   *is seated, holding the baby, with BRIAN looking on. For a moment,*
21   *everything stops. Then the WOMEN VILLAGERS sing "Rocking"*
22   *[or one of the other medieval lullaby tunes, such as "The Coventry*
23   *Carol," "The Chester Carol" or even "Away in a Manger"].)*
24   *SONG:*   "Rocking."
25   **WOMAN VILLAGERS:**   *(Singing)* **Little Jesus, sweetly sleep,**
26   **do not stir;**
27   **We will lend a coat of fur,**
28
29   **We will rock you, rock you, rock you,**
30   **We will rock you, rock you, rock you.**
31
32   **See the fur to keep you warm,**
33   **Snugly round your tiny form.**
34
35   **Mary's little baby, sleep, sweetly sleep,**

1   **Sleep in comfort, slumber deep,**

2

3   **We will rock you, rock you, rock you,**

4   **We will rock you, rock you, rock you.**

5

6   **We will serve you all we can,**

7   **Darling, darling little man.**

8   **DUNLEY: But the story needed to be told. People needed to**
9   **hear it.** *(MIKE and DENNIS rush on from behind the wagon.*
10   *They're dressed like rustics again.)* **So, while shepherds**
11   **watched their flock by night** . . . *(DENNIS pulls on MIKE's*
12   *sleeve. He points up at the huge medieval sun above the cathedral*
13   *doors.)*
14   **MIKE: He said we're watching this by** *night,* **knave!** *(The*
15   *MOON-AND-SUN PUPPETEER pops his head above the*
16   *cathedral doors.)*
17   **PUPPETEER: Sorry!** *(The huge medieval sun drops down and the*
18   *moon comes up. The lights change to night colors. Suddenly, the*
19   *NIGHT WATCHMAN comes racing in, tugging on his hat and*
20   *tolling his bell. He stops and sees the VILLAGERS staring at*
21   *him. He scratches his head, confused. He stomps off, mumbling*
22   *to himself. MIKE nods at DUNLEY to continue.)*
23   **DUNLEY: So, while shepherds watched their flock by** *night,*
24   **the angel of the Lord came upon them.** *(Suddenly the*
25   *VILLAGERS sing the opening lines of "Hark! the Herald Angels*
26   *Sing" a cappella and very loud. DENNIS and MIKE almost*
27   *jump out of their skins. They look up.)*
28   **DENNIS: And the glory of the Lord shone round about them —**
29   **MIKE: *(Cutting in)* And they were terrified.** *(To the audience)* **In**
30   **fact, one of the shepherds was so scared that he ran across**
31   **the fields and he fell down this ravine and broke his leg**
32   **in three places —** *(DENNIS taps his shoulder. MIKE stops.*
33   *He rolls his eyes and gestures for DUNLEY to resume telling*
34   *the story.)*
35   **DUNLEY: But the angel said** . . . *(Jumps up on a stump.)* **"Don't**

1   **be afraid. I'm bringing you glad tidings of great joy which**
2   **shall be for all people. Tonight in Bethlehem a Savior**
3   **has been born. He is Christ the Lord. And this will be a**
4   **sign to you: You'll find the baby wrapped in strips of cloth**
5   **and lying in a manger." And suddenly the night sky was**
6   **filled with the heavenly host singing, "Glory to God in**
7   **the highest, and on earth, peace to those on whom his**
8   **favor rests!"** *(MIKE is staring up at DUNLEY in awe. He wipes*
9   *a tear away.)*
10 **MIKE:**   **I love that part. It gets me every time.**
11 **DENNIS:**   **Sort of tells the whole story, doesn't it?** *(DENNIS*
12   *and MIKE run to the wagon.)*
13 **MIKE:**   **And so they went, and found Mary and Joseph. And**
14   **the baby, who was lying in a manger! And the shepherds**
15   **returned, glorifying God for all the things they had seen**
16   **and heard.**
17 **DENNIS:**   **Which happened.**
18 **MIKE:**   **Just as they had been told.** *(DUNLEY gives him a look.)*
19   **Exactly.** *(He sees the VILLAGERS staring at him.)* **Word for**
20   **word.** *(Another look from DUNLEY.)* **With *no* changes.** *(The*
21   *VILLAGERS cheer. The SOLOIST, dressed as a traveling*
22   *troubadour, suddenly breaks through the crowd and begins*
23   *singing a song about the angels. [The original production used*
24   *"Glory" by Mary Rice Hopkins.] A carol sing can follow here, if*
25   *desired. The choir director may direct the audience to stand and*
26   *sing familiar carols, beginning with "Angels We Have Heard on*
27   *HIgh" or "The First Noel." At the close of the carol sing, the*
28   *VILLAGERS cheer and shake hands with DUNLEY and the*
29   *ACTORS. The ACTORS hop up into their wagon. They wave*
30   *to the VILLAGERS.)*
31 **DUNLEY:**   **Thanks, friends, for helping us tell the Christmas**
32   **story!**
33 **MIKE:**   ***The* Christmas story. You mean, *our* Christmas story.**
34   *(DUNLEY grins and nods.)* **Farewell!**
35 **OLIVE:**   **Farewell, villagers of _____!** *(Your town name*

1   *here)* **Perhaps we can perform for you once again.**

2   **BRIAN:**   Hey, I've got this great idea for an Easter pageant.

3   **DENNIS:**   You do?

4   **BRIAN:**   **Yeah, but we're going to have to find some live**

5   **elephants!** *(MIKE, DENNIS and BRIAN pull the curtains*

6   *closed in OLIVE's face. She jumps down off the wagon and*

7   *stomps her foot.)*

8   **OLIVE:**   **Elephants, huh?** *(She grabs the wagon hitch.)* **Great!**

9   **Maybe we can get one of 'em to pull this thing!** *(The lights*

10   *go out on the wagon. In the darkness, we hear the wagon pull*

11   *away.)*

12

13

14

15

16

17

18

19

20

21

22

23

24

25

26

27

28

29

30

31

32

33

34

35

1   **SCENE SEVEN**

2

3   *(The lights come up on the VILLAGERS. They're all surrounding*

4   *DUNLEY, shaking his hand and clapping him on the shoulder.)*

5 **VILLAGER ONE:**   **What do you think?**

6 **VILLAGER TWO:**   **Is he the one?**

7 **VILLAGER THREE:**   **Let us make this young man our new**

8   **parson!** *(A cheer goes up. DUNLEY is grinning from ear to ear.*

9   *Then OLD MAN WINTER makes his way through the crowd,*

10   *mumbling and whacking people out of the way with his staff.*

11   *He breaks to the front of the stage.)*

12 **OLD MAN WINTER:**   **Now hold on a doggone minute!** *(The*

13   *VILLAGERS are shocked. They ad-lib whispers: "Old Man*

14   *Winter!" "He's talking!" "He's not crazy after all!")*

15 **OLD MAN WINTER:**   *(To DUNLEY)* **OK, whippersnapper, let**

16   **me see your resume.**

17 **DUNLEY:**   **My resume?**

18 **OLD MAN WINTER:**   **You do have a resume, don't ya?!**

19   *(DUNLEY looks at the audience and smiles.)*

20 **DUNLEY:**   **I thought they'd never ask!** *(DUNLEY unfurls a*

21   *huge scroll. It rolls to the ground, and then some. OLD MAN*

22   *WINTER looks amazed. He takes the scroll and begins to read*

23   *it over. The VILLAGERS lean in toward him, hanging on every*

24   *sound.)*

25 **OLD MAN WINTER:**   *(Reading)* **Hmmm . . . I don't know . . .**

26   **let me see here. Good preaching skills . . . hmmm . . . well,**

27   **now . . . tch, tch, tch. A little weak on administration . . .**

28   *(He suddenly turns and looks at DUNLEY.)* **When can ya start,**

29   **whippersnapper?!** *(The VILLAGERS cheer. They begin to*

30   *chant "Dun-ley! Dun-ley! Dun-ley!" They push him up the*

31   *cathedral steps right to the cathedral doors. DUNLEY beams a*

32   *smile and invites one of the ELDERLY VILLAGE WOMEN to*

33   *open the padlock. She steps up, flexes her arms — and pulls the*

34   *huge lock off the doors! A cheer goes up. OLD MAN WINTER*

35   *tosses the resume.)*

1   **Well, my job's done. Let's eat!** *(Another cheer goes up.*
2   *From the aisle, a SOLOIST begins singing "The Boar's Head*
3   *Carol." He is dressed in a butcher's apron and wears a festive*
4   *wreath on his head. He also carries a huge platter covered in*
5   *holly. An actual boar's head is optional. The SOLOIST is*
6   *followed by two VILLAGERS with large baskets of breads, meats,*
7   *fruits and cheeses.)*
8 *SONG:* "The Boar's Head Carol."
9 **SOLOIST:** *(Singing)* **The boar's head in hand bear I,**
10   **Bedecked with bays and rosemary;**
11   **And I pray you, my masters, be merry,**
12   **Quot estis in convivio:**
13
14   **Caput apri defero,**
15   **Reddens laudes Domino.**
16
17   **The boar's head, as I understand,**
18   **Is the rarest dish in all the land**
19   **When thus bedecked with a gay garland,**
20   **Let us servire cantico:**
21 *CHORUS:* **Our steward hath provided this**
22   **In honor of the King of bliss,**
23   **Which on this day to be served is,**
24   **In reginensi atrio.**
25   *(Repeat chorus.)*
26   *(Then the VILLAGERS break into "Deck the Halls.")*
27 *SONG:* "Deck the Halls."
28 **VILLAGERS:** *(Singing)* **Deck the halls with boughs of holly,**
29   **Fa la la la la, la la la la.**
30   **'Tis the season to be jolly,**
31   **Fa la la la la, la la la la.**
32   **Don we now our gay apparel,**
33   **Fa la la la la, la la la la.**
34   **Troll the ancient Yuletide carol,**
35   **Fa la la la la, la la la la.**

1	See the blazing Yule before us,
2	Fa la la la la, la la la la.
3	Strike the harp and join the chorus,
4	Fa la la la la, la la la la.
5	Follow me in merry measure,
6	Fa la la la la, la la la la.
7	While I tell of Christmas treasure,
8	Fa la la la la, la la la la.
9	
10	Fast away the old year passes,
11	Fa la la la la, la la la la.
12	Hail the new, ye lads and lasses,
13	Fa la la la la, la la la la.
14	Sing we joyous all together,
15	Fa la la la la, la la la la.
16	Heedless of the wind or weather,
17	Fa la la la la, la la la la.
18	*(The VILLAGERS turn to the audience.)*
19	**VILLAGERS:** Merry Christmas!
20	*(The VILLAGERS process out into the aisles, singing "We Wish*
21	*You a Merry Christmas.")*
22	*SONG:* "We Wish You a Merry Christmas."
23	**VILLAGERS:** *(Singing)* **We wish you a merry Christmas,**
24	**We wish you a merry Christmas,**
25	**We wish you a merry Christmas,**
26	**And a happy new year!**
27	
28	**Good tidings we bring**
29	**To you and your kin,**
30	**Good tidings for Christmas**
31	**And a happy new year!**
32	
33	**We wish you a merry Christmas,**
34	**We wish you a merry Christmas,**
35	**We wish you a merry Christmas,**

1   And a happy new year!
2
3   Now bring us the figgy pudding,
4   Now bring us the figgy pudding,
5   Now bring us the figgy pudding,
6   And bring some right here!
7
8   We wish you a merry Christmas,
9   We wish you a merry Christmas,
10   We wish you a merry Christmas,
11   And a happy new year!
12
13   For we all love our figgy pudding,
14   We all love our figgy pudding,
15   We all love our figgy pudding,
16   So bring some out here!
17
18   And we won't go until we get some,
19   We won't go until we get some,
20   We won't go until we get some,
21   So bring some out here!
22
23   We wish you a merry Christmas,
24   We wish you a merry Christmas,
25   We wish you a merry Christmas,
26   And a happy new year!
27   *(The VILLAGERS finish the song in the back of the sanctuary.*
28   *The lights come down to night colors on the stage. The medieval*
29   *moon rises. The NIGHT WATCHMAN tolls his bell from Off-*
30   *stage.)*
31   **NIGHT WATCHMAN:** *(Off-stage)* **Three o'clock and all is**
32   **well! Three o'clock and all is well!** *(He walks out onto the*
33   *empty stage.)* **Three o'clock and all is ...** *(He sees the*
34   *audience.)* **Do you people know what time it is? You should**
35   **be in bed! Listen, why don't you come back next Sunday?**

1   **I hear the new parson is preaching.** *(The NIGHT*
2   *WATCHMAN goes out tolling the bell as the lights go to*
3   *blackout.)*
4
5
6
7
8
9
10
11
12
13
14
15
16
17
18
19
20
21
22
23
24
25
26
27
28
29
30
31
32
33
34
35

CANDLES AND CAROLS

A Church
Family Celebration
for
Christmas Eve

L. G. Enscoe
Annie Enscoe

Lisa Loomis (L), Laura Hill and Eric Loomis in *Candles and Carols.*

CANDLES AND CAROLS

CAST

FIRST VOICE
A man or woman

SECOND VOICE
A woman

THIRD VOICE
A man or woman

MAN

WOMAN

MARY

JOSEPH

SHEPHERD ONE
A man or woman

SHEPHERD TWO
A man or woman

SHEPHERD THREE
A man or woman

MAGUS ONE

MAGUS TWO

MAGUS THREE

MINISTER or SPEAKER

MEMBER ONE
A man or woman from the congregation

191

CAST
(Continued)

MEMBER TWO
A man or woman from the congregation

MEMBER THREE
A man or woman from the congregation

CHOIR

CHILDREN'S CHOIR

MEN'S TRIO

PRODUCTION NOTES

Running Time

One hour to seventy minutes.

Props

Candles (three candles surrounding one large candle plus many small candles to be placed in the pews). A Nativity set (with stable and figures). This can be a traditional size set or larger. Earthen jug; two sawhorses; wooden chair; wooden plank (wide enough to accommodate Joseph lying on it); brown cloth; a manger (actual size); Christ child (doll); straw; basket; star chart rolled like a scroll; shepherds' gifts (milk, cheese, bread); wise men gifts (gold, frankincense, myrrh); optional gifts for clergy, staff, choir members, etc.

Costumes

The Choir can be dressed in choir robes or clothes in jewel tones or deeper traditional Christmas colors. Nothing should be bright.

The Voices are dressed in dark clothes, which can be added to later in the program with a brighter jacket, or sweater or scarf to signify the light in the darkness. Also needed is a rugged, torn cloak and a bright, kingly robe for Second Voice.

The biblical characters are dressed in traditional clothes. These can be found in your pageant closet, or rented from a local costume store, or made from Bible-character patterns that usually come out during the holidays, or you might choose to create a more contemporary stylized version of the biblical clothes.

Set

The sanctuary platform should be cleared. The Choir sings from the risers. The Voices can speak from anywhere in the sanctuary. No lectern or podium is required. All locations (i.e. Joseph's shop, Bethlehem, the stable) should only be pantomimed. No sets are required for these.

SUGGESTED MUSIC SOURCES

The musical selections for "Candles and Carols" can be found in most hymnals.

"O Come, O Come, Emmanuel," "Lo, How a Rose E'er Blooming," "Come, Thou Long-Expected Jesus," "Of the Father's Love Begotten," "O Little Town of Bethlehem," "Away in a Manger," "Thou Didst Leave Thy Throne," "Silent Night," "The First Noel," "Hark! the Herald Angels Sing," "Angels We Have Heard on High," "We Three Kings," "I Wonder As I Wander," "Joy to the World," and "O Come All Ye Faithful" may be found in *Hymns for the Family of God,* published by Paragon Associates, Nashville, Tennessee, 1976.

"Comfort Ye My People," "In the Bleak Midwinter," "What Child Is This?" and "Brightest and Best" may be found in *The Hymnal 1982* of the Episcopal Church, the Church Hymnal Corporation, New York, 1985.

"The Magnificat" is the author's own paraphrase of Mary's words. Original music can be written, or other musical versions of the Magnificat can be used.

AUTHORS' NOTES

Candles and Carols is a traditional family Christmas service — complete with carols, hymns, Scripture readings and short dramatic moments. It's designed to be a worship time for the whole body, with clergy, choir and congregation as part of the program.

The idea was to create a celebration time that can be effective with little funds, limited resources, and simple staging.

The quotations from Scripture were designed by the authors. You may wish to use a version more familiar to your congregation. Unless otherwise indicated, the Scripture is taken from Matthew and Luke.

Traditional Christmas carols and hymns were chosen for the music — pieces that can be found in the hymnal or with little effort. If more music or alternate choices are desired — perhaps if a choir director wants to challenge his or her choir with less-familiar choral works — room is left for those kinds of alterations. Break out the Rutter and Shaw catalogs!

We are pleased to offer a worshipful evening that incorporates the whole Gospel, from Bethlehem to Calvary — along with all the familiar elements that make Christmas such a bright season. A season of hope. A season of new birth.

CANDLES AND CAROLS

A Church
Family Celebration
for
Christmas Eve

INTRO
"The Light of the World"

FIRST VERSE
"The Longing for the Light"

SECOND VERSE
"Mary and Gabriel"

THIRD VERSE
"Joseph Sees the Light"

CHORUS
"In Thy Dark Streets Shineth"

FOURTH VERSE
"The Shepherds and the Angels"

FIFTH VERSE
"Star of Wonder"

TO CODA
"Come, Thou Long-Expected Jesus"

1	**INTRO**
2	"The Light of the World"
3	
4	*(The sanctuary is half lit. Music is playing as the congregation*
5	*enters — hymns and carols of mourning and longing for God.*
6	*Appropriate selections may be found in the "Advent" section of*
7	*your hymnal. No Christmas carols yet.*
8	*(The sanctuary platform is empty of furniture, except pews or*
9	*risers for the CHOIR. Christmas greenery is fine, but no bright*
10	*colors or decorations.*
11	*(On one side of the platform is an empty Nativity stable. The*
12	*figures may be hidden behind it. On the other side — or*
13	*somewhere else on the platform — are three candles surrounding*
14	*one large candle: Christ, the Light of the World. Small candles*
15	*have been placed in the pews.*
16	*(The setting is very somber, with no hint of the joy and celebration*
17	*of Christmas to come.*
18	*(FIRST VOICE comes in, dressed in dark clothes. He, and the*
19	*other VOICES, speak from various places throughout the*
20	*sanctuary.)*
21	**FIRST VOICE:** **Christmas is nearly here.**
22	**A time to give.**
23	**Give to our families, to our friends,**
24	**To those around us in need.**
25	**It's a time to give the world a**
26	**Lighted vision of life and hope.**
27	**A vision it might not see with**
28	**Such brightness. Until now.**
29	*(SECOND VOICE enters, dressed in dark clothes.)*
30	**SECOND VOICE:** **Christmas is nearly here.**
31	**A time to understand.**
32	**Understand what we have been given.**
33	**A gift so precious —**
34	**So rare,**
35	**So beyond what we could have ever**

1	Asked for,
2	That once we receive it,
3	How can our lives ever be the same?
4	*(THIRD VOICE enters, dressed as the others.)*
5	THIRD VOICE: Christmas is nearly here.
6	A time to remember.
7	Remember the aching emptiness of a world
8	Crying out.
9	And the passion of a God who
10	Answered.
11	And the forever joy — offered to a
12	People who once believed God's only
13	Gifts were:
14	Anger
15	Suffering
16	And distant silence.
17	*(A single woodwind or stringed instrument begins a slow, sparse*
18	*and mournful rendition of "O Come, O Come, Emmanuel.")*
19	FIRST VOICE: Christmas is nearly here.
20	Tonight we want to celebrate
21	A dark night
22	That lit up history
23	From dawn to dusk.
24	We want words and music rejoicing
25	In the promise fulfilled.
26	A savior. Jesus Christ.
27	Born to us.
28	Born to die.
29	Born to give us second birth.
30	SECOND VOICE: Tonight we will sing our own carol of
31	sadness turned to joy.
32	THIRD VOICE: Shadows to light.
33	FIRST VOICE: Silence to celebration.
34	*(The VOICES go out. The lights in the sanctuary come up a*
35	*little. The CHOIR enters from the back, singing "O Come, O*

1 *Come, Emmanuel." They process down the aisles toward their*
2 *positions on the platform. The CHOIR may invite the*
3 *congregation to sing the final verse with them.)*
4 **SONG:** "O Come, O Come, Emmanuel."
5 **CHOIR:** *(Singing)* **O come, O come, Emmanuel,**
6 **And ransom captive Israel,**
7 **That mourns in lonely exile here,**
8 **Until the Son of God appear.**
9
10 **Rejoice! Rejoice! Emmanuel**
11 **Shall come to thee, O Israel!**
12
13 **O come, thou Dayspring, come and cheer**
14 **Our spirits by thine advent here,**
15 **Disperse the gloomy clouds of night,**
16 **And death's dark shadows put to flight.**
17
18 **Rejoice! Rejoice! Emmanuel**
19 **Shall come to thee, O Israel!**
20
21 **O come, thou Wisdom from on high,**
22 **And order all things far and nigh,**
23 **To us the path of knowledge show,**
24 **And cause us in her ways to go.**
25
26 **Rejoice! Rejoice! Emmanuel**
27 **Shall come to thee, O Israel!**
28
29 **O come, Desire of nations, bind**
30 **In one the hearts of all mankind,**
31 **Bid thou our sad divisions cease,**
32 **And be thyself our King of peace.**
33
34 **Rejoice! Rejoice! Emmanuel**
35 **Shall come to thee, O Israel!**

1	*(At the close of the hymn, the pianist continues playing as the*
2	*lights in the sanctuary fade out.)*
3	
4	
5	
6	
7	
8	
9	
10	
11	
12	
13	
14	
15	
16	
17	
18	
19	
20	
21	
22	
23	
24	
25	
26	
27	
28	
29	
30	
31	
32	
33	
34	
35	

1   **FIRST VERSE**

FIRST VERSE
"The Longing for the Light"

(A light comes up on the FIRST VOICE.)

FIRST VOICE: **"The Longing for the Light."** *(The MINISTER can either join FIRST VOICE or speak from another place on the platform.)*

MINISTER: Open your eyes. "A time is coming," says the Lord, "when I will create a new covenant with the house of Israel and the house of Judah. It will be nothing like the covenant I made with their ancestors when I took hold of their hands and led them out of Egypt. A covenant they shattered to pieces — even though I loved them like a husband," says the Lord. (Jeremiah 31:31-32)

(The music begins for the hymn "Comfort, Comfort Now My People." SECOND and THIRD VOICES return. They kneel on the platform, facing the congregation.)

FIRST VOICE: O God, you have pushed us away and broken us. You have been angry. Oh, take us back to you again.

SECOND VOICE: You have shaken the earth and torn it open. Heal up the cracks, for it is crumbling.

THIRD VOICE: You have made us drink bitterness. You have given us wine that makes us stagger.

FIRST VOICE: Yet you have set up a banner for those who love you. A place of escape before danger falls.

SECOND VOICE: Save those who are dear to you. Answer your loved ones with liberation. (Psalm 60:1-5)

(The CHOIR sings "Comfort, Comfort Now My People." The VOICES exit.)

SONG: "Comfort, Comfort Now My People."

CHOIR: *(Singing)* **Comfort, comfort now my people;**
Speak of peace: so say our God.
Comfort those who sit in darkness,
Mourning under sorrow's load.

Cry out to Jerusalem

1   Of the peace that awaits for them;
2   Tell her that her sins
3   I cover and her warfare now is over.
4
5   For the herald's voice is crying
6   In the desert far and near,
7   Calling all to true repentance,
8   Since the kingdom now is here.
9
10   Oh, that warning cry obey!
11   Now prepare for God a way!
12   Let the valleys rise to meet him,
13   And the hills bow down to greet him.
14
15   Then make straight what long was crooked;
16   Make the rougher places plain.
17   Let your hearts be true and humble,
18   As befits his holy reign.
19
20   For the glory of the Lord
21   Now on earth is shed abroad,
22   And all flesh shall see the token
23   That God's word is never broken.
24   *(When the hymn is done, SECOND VOICE enters from the back*
25   *of the sanctuary dressed in a rugged, torn cloak. She strides up*
26   *the aisle.)*
27   **SECOND VOICE:**   *(Passionately)* **A voice is calling! "Clear out a**
28   **way for the Lord in the wilderness! Make a smooth**
29   **highway in the desert for our God. Let every valley be**
30   **raised up and every mountain and hill be leveled. Let**
31   **the rough ground become plain, and the rugged earth an**
32   **open valley. Then God's glory will be displayed. And all**
33   **humanity will see it together. For the mouth of God has**
34   **promised it."** (Isaiah 40:3-5)
35   *(The other VOICES have come in during her words, listening*

1   *to her. THIRD VOICE turns to the congregation.)*
2   **THIRD VOICE:** **And the words of God spoken through the**
3   **prophets began to create a dim, distant portrait of the**
4   **one we were to look for.** *(The pianist plays "Redeemer of the*
5   *Nations, Come," [or an Advent hymn of your choice] softly beneath*
6   *the following verses. MEMBERS OF THE CONGREGATION, in*
7   *turn, stand and offer their verses.)*
8   **MEMBER ONE:** **"For this reason, the Lord himself will give**
9   **you a sign. Look, a virgin is with child, and she will give**
10   **birth to a son. And she will give him the name**
11   **'Immanuel.' "** (Isaiah 7:14)
12   **MEMBER TWO:** **"But as for you, Bethlehem Ephratha, too**
13   **small to be counted among the cities of Judah, out of you**
14   **will come a ruler for me in Israel. One whose beginnings**
15   **are from old, from ancient days."** (Micah 5:2)
16   **MEMBER THREE:** **"For a child will be born to us. To us, a**
17   **son will be given. And the government will lean on his**
18   **shoulder. And his name will be called Wonderful**
19   **Counselor —"**
20   **MEMBER ONE:** **"Mighty God."**
21   **MEMBER TWO:** **"Eternal Father."**
22   **MEMBER THREE:** **"Prince of Peace."** (Isaiah 9:6)
23   *(The pianist begins playing the opening of "Lo! How a Rose E'er*
24   *Blooming.")*
25   **FIRST VOICE:** *(Over music)* **"Listen. The days are coming**
26   **says the Lord, when I will raise up for David a righteous**
27   **Branch. And he shall reign as king and deal wisely, and**
28   **shall execute justice and righteousness in the land."**
29   (Jeremiah 23:5)
30   *(VOICES exit. The CHOIR sings a choral presentation of "Lo!*
31   *How a Rose E'er Blooming.")*
32   *SONG:* "Lo! How a Rose E'er Blooming."
33   **CHOIR:** *(Singing)* **Lo! how a rose e'er blooming**
34   **From tender stem hath sprung!**
35   **Of Jesse's lineage coming**

1	As men of old have sung.
2	
3	It came, a flower bright,
4	Amid the cold of winter,
5	When half-gone was the night.
6	
7	Isaiah 'twas foretold it,
8	The rose I have in mind;
9	With Mary we behold it,
10	The virgin mother kind.
11	
12	To show God's love aright
13	She bore to men a Savior,
14	When half-gone was the night.
15	
16	This flower, whose fragrance tender
17	With sweetness fills the air,
18	Dispels with glorious splendor
19	The darkness everywhere.
20	
21	True man, yet very God,
22	From sin and death he saves us,
23	And lightens every load.
24	*(The CHOIR and CONGREGATION then sing "Come, Thou*
25	*Long-Expected Jesus.")*
26	*SONG:* "Come, Thou Long-Expected Jesus."
27	**CHOIR/CONGREGATION:** *(Singing)* **Come, thou long-expected**
28	**Jesus,**
29	**Born to set thy people free;**
30	**From our fears and sins release us;**
31	**Let us find our rest in thee.**
32	
33	**Israel's strength and consolation,**
34	**Hope of all the earth thou art;**
35	**Dear desire of every nation,**

1   Joy of every longing heart.
2
3   Born thy people to deliver,
4   Born a child and yet a King,
5   Born to reign in us forever,
6   Now thy gracious Kingdom bring.
7
8   By thine own eternal spirit
9   Rule in all our hearts alone;
10   By thine all-sufficient merit,
11   Raise us to thy glorious throne.
12
13
14
15
16
17
18
19
20
21
22
23
24
25
26
27
28
29
30
31
32
33
34
35

1   **SECOND VERSE**
2   "Mary and Gabriel"
3

4 *(At the close of the hymn, the FIRST VOICE enters. He lights*
5 *the first candle.)*
6 **FIRST VOICE:** **"Mary and Gabriel."** *(FIRST VOICE exits. The*
7 *CHOIR sits — except for MAN and WOMAN, who remain*
8 *standing. The CHOIR continues humming the previous hymn*
9 *[or another choice]. It rises in intensity. MARY enters, either in*
10 *traditional biblical costume or something contemporary and*
11 *stylized. She's carrying an earthen jug. It's heavy. She sets it*
12 *down and straightens out her tired back.)*
13 **MAN:** **In the sixth month, God sent the angel Gabriel to**
14 **Nazareth, a city in Galilee.**
15 **WOMAN:** **To a young woman engaged to be married to a man**
16 **named Joseph, of the house of David. The young woman's**
17 **name was Mary.** *(MARY bends down and picks up the jar.*
18 *She starts to move on. The CHOIR suddenly stops humming.*
19 *MARY stops in her tracks. Something's odd. She turns around.*
20 *She sees Gabriel [invisible to us]. She gasps.)*
21 **CHOIR WOMEN:** *(Pianissimo)* **Hello, Mary. How favored you**
22 **are! The Lord is with you!** *(MARY backs away, astounded*
23 *and terrified.)*
24 **WOMAN:** *(Urgently)* **Mary was disturbed by the angel's words.**
25 **She could only wonder what this kind of greeting might**
26 **mean.**
27 **MAN:** **But the angel said to her:**
28 **CHOIR WOMEN:** *(Pianissimo)* **Don't be afraid, Mary. You have**
29 **found favor with God! Listen, you will conceive in your womb**
30 **and give birth to a son. You will call his name Jesus.**
31 *(The following lines overlap each other, delivered by individual*
32 *CHOIR WOMEN. The CHOIR MEN begin a low hum, rising*
33 *in intensity.)*
34 **CHOIR WOMEN:** *(Individually, overlapping)* **He will be called**
35 **great.**

1	**He will be called the Son of the Most High.**
2	**The Lord God will give him the throne of King David.**
3	**He will reign over the house of Jacob forever.**
4	**His kingdom will have no end.**
5	**WOMAN:** And Mary said to the angel:
6	**MARY:** How can all this be? I have had no relations with a
7	man.
8	**MAN:** And the angel said:
9	**CHOIR WOMEN:** *(Pianissimo)* **The Holy Spirit will come to**
10	**you. The power of God will overshadow you. The child**
11	**born will be called holy, the Son of God.** *(MARY steps back,*
12	*shocked and frightened. WOMAN comes to MARY and puts her*
13	*arms around her, comforting her.)* **Listen. Your cousin**
14	**Elizabeth has conceived a son in her old age. This is the**
15	**sixth month for a woman once called barren.**
16	**WOMAN:** Mary, nothing God says is impossible. *(MARY*
17	*struggles with the news, afraid, confused, and honored.)*
18	**WOMAN:** And Mary said:
19	**MARY:** I am the servant of the Lord. I want it to happen to me
20	just as you have said. *(Pause)*
21	**MAN:** And the angel went away. *(MAN and WOMAN return to*
22	*the CHOIR. MARY starts to pick up the jar. Suddenly the power*
23	*of the message overcomes her. She nearly drops it.)*
24	**MARY:** *(Whispering)* **I am ... the servant of the Lord. I want**
25	**it to happen ... just as you have said.** *(She sings or says*
26	*"The Magnificat." Other musical versions may be used here.)*
27	*SONG:* "The Magnificat."
28	**MARY:** *(Singing or saying)* **My soul sings out the greatness of**
29	**the Lord!**
30	**My spirit rejoices in God my Savior.**
31	**His eyes searched out**
32	**This simple servant girl.**
33	**My spirit sings out to God my Savior!**
34	
35	**From this moment, honor will cover me.**

1   Holy is his name, age to age the same.
2   Great things he has done for me.
3   Holy his name, merciful hand stretched to save
4   Those who trust and bless his name.
5
6   Arrogant hearts he has pushed aside,
7   The rich he has put to flight.
8   But the humble he has lifted high,
9   The hungry he will satisfy.
10
11 My soul sings out the greatness of the Lord!
12 My spirit rejoices in God my Savior.
13 His eyes searched out
14 This simple servant girl.
15 My spirit sings out to God my Savior!
16 *(MARY moves off the platform. She stays in view, but turns her*
17 *back to the congregation. The MAN and WOMAN move off or*
18 *back into the CHOIR.)*
19
20
21
22
23
24
25
26
27
28
29
30
31
32
33
34
35

THIRD VERSE

"Joseph Sees the Light"

(The pianist plays "O Come, O Come, Emmanuel," softly. FIRST VOICE enters and lights the second candle.)

FIRST VOICE: **"Joseph Sees the Light."** *(SECOND VOICE and THIRD VOICE enter. They each carry a sawhorse. One of them is also carrying a wooden chair. They set them in the center of the platform as SECOND VOICE talks.)*

SECOND VOICE: **When Mary, Jesus' mother, had been pledged to be married to Joseph, but before they came to live together, she was found to be with child — by the Holy Spirit.** *(JOSEPH comes in, carrying a wide plank of wood. He sets it on the sawhorses and mimes working, prepping the lumber. MARY turns around. She steps onto the platform. JOSEPH looks up and sees her standing there. He stops working. They stare at one another.)*

THIRD VOICE: **And Joseph, being a just man and unwilling to subject her to public shame, resolved to send her away quietly.** *(The pianist stops. MARY slowly turns her back to him. JOSEPH watches her, sadly. He drops his head in his hands. He is emotionally weary. The lights fade to night colors as JOSEPH climbs up on the wood and lays back.)*

SECOND VOICE: **But as he considered this, an angel of the Lord appeared to him in a dream:**

CHOIR MEN: *(Pianissimo)* **Joseph, son of David. Don't be afraid to take Mary as your wife. The child inside her is of the Holy Spirit. She will give birth to a son. You will give him the name Jesus, for he will save the people from their sins.** *(JOSEPH awakes during these words. He sits up.)*

JOSEPH: **All this is happening to fulfill what God said through the prophet: "Listen, a virgin will conceive and have a son, and his name will be called Emmanuel. Emmanuel. God with us."**

FIRST VOICE: **When Joseph woke from his sleep, he did as**

1   **the angel of the Lord had told him.** *(JOSEPH goes to MARY.*

2   *She turns to him. He takes her hand.)* **He took her home to**

3   **be his wife, but he had no relations with her before she**

4   **gave birth to a son.**

5   **MARY:**   **And he called his name Jesus.** *(The CHOIR sings "Of*

6   *the Father's Love Begotten." During the hymn, MARY and*

7   *JOSEPH place the Mary, Joseph, and baby Jesus figures in the*

8   *empty stable, then they and the VOICES exit.)*

9   *SONG:*   "Of the Father's Love Begotten."

10   **CHOIR:**   *(Singing)* **Of the Father's love begotten,**

11   **Ere the worlds began to be,**

12   **He is Alpha and Omega,**

13   **He the source, the ending he;**

14   **Of the things that are, that have been,**

15   **And that future years shall see,**

16   **Evermore and evermore!**

17

18   **O ye heights of heaven, adore him;**

19   **Angel hosts, his praises sing;**

20   **Powers, dominions bow before him,**

21   **And extol our God and King;**

22   **Let no tongue on earth be silent,**

23   **Every voice in concert ring,**

24   **Evermore and evermore!**

25

26   **Christ, to thee with God the Father,**

27   **And, O Holy Ghost, to thee,**

28   **Hymn and chant and high thanksgiving,**

29   **And unwearied praises be:**

30   **Honor, glory and dominion,**

31   **And eternal victory,**

32   **Evermore and evermore!**

33   *(At the close of the hymn, the lights slowly fade out on the*

34   *platform.)*

35

1 **CHORUS**
2 "In Thy Dark Streets Shineth"
3
4 *(The pianist plays "O Little Town of Bethlehem" softly. FIRST*
5 *VOICE enters. He lights the third candle. When he is through:)*
6 **FIRST VOICE:** **"In Thy Dark Streets Shineth."** *(Lights come up*
7 *on the center platform. FIRST VOICE grabs the wooden chair*
8 *and sits behind the sawhorses and plank as if it were a table.*
9 *SECOND VOICE, THIRD VOICE, MARY and JOSEPH enter*
10 *and line up to one side of it.)* **During that time, a decree went**
11 **out from Caesar Augustus commanding that a census be**
12 **taken of the entire world. So all went to be enrolled, each**
13 **one to his ancestral city.** *(FIRST VOICE pounds the table.*
14 *SECOND VOICE steps up and mimes signing a book. THIRD*
15 *VOICE follows with the same business.)*
16 **SECOND VOICE:** **So Joseph went up from Galilee, from the**
17 **city of Nazareth, to Judea, to the city of David, called**
18 **Bethlehem, because he was of the house and lineage of**
19 **David.**
20 **THIRD VOICE:** **He went to be enrolled with Mary, his promised**
21 **wife, who was with child.**
22 **JOSEPH:** **And while they were there, the time came for the**
23 **baby to be born.** *(The CHOIR sings "O Little Town of*
24 *Bethlehem." A SOLOIST can sing the first verse. During the*
25 *carol, the VOICES move the wooden chair and sawhorses aside,*
26 *setting them end to end. They drape a ragged brown cloth over*
27 *the horses, making a small backdrop. This is now the "stable."*
28 *An empty manger is placed in front. The VOICES exit.)*
29 ***SONG:*** "O Little Town of Bethlehem."
30 **SOLOIST:** *(Singing)* **O little town of Bethlehem,**
31 **How still we see thee lie!**
32 **Above thy deep and dreamless sleep**
33 **The silent stars go by;**
34 **Yet in thy dark streets shineth**
35 **The everlasting Light;**

1   The hopes and fears of all the years
2   Are met in thee tonight.
3   CHOIR: *(Singing)* For Christ is born of Mary,
4   And gathered all above,
5   While mortals sleep, the angels keep
6   Their watch of wondering love.
7   O morning stars, together
8   Proclaim the holy birth!
9   And praises sing to God the King,
10   And peace to men on earth!
11
12   How silently, how silently,
13   The wondrous gift is given!
14   So God imparts to human hearts
15   The blessings of his heaven.
16   No ear may hear his coming,
17   But in this world of sin,
18   Where meek souls will receive him, still
19   The dear Christ enters in.
20
21   O holy child of Bethlehem!
22   Descend to us, we pray;
23   Cast out our sin and enter in,
24   Be born in us today.
25   We hear the Christmas angels
26   The great glad tidings tell;
27   O come to us, abide with us,
28   Our Lord Emmanuel!
29   *(JOSEPH and MARY appraoch the stable. He stops MARY*
30   *outside, then ducks inside and looks around. It hurts his feelings*
31   *that this is the only place he could find. He quickly kneels down*
32   *and pantomimes pushing rocks and filth out of the way. JOSEPH*
33   *goes out and tenderly leads MARY inside and helps her lie down.*
34   *He takes off his coat and puts it under her head. Her time is near.*
35   *He looks around, anxiously. Then he sees the manger. He freezes.*

1   *(The lights fade on the stable — except for a light on the manger.*
2   *A SOLOIST sings "In the Bleak Midwinter," accompanied only*
3   *with a guitar.)*
4   **SONG:**   "In the Bleak Midwinter."
5   **SOLOIST:**   *(Singing)* **In the bleak midwinter,**
6   **Frosty wind made moan.**
7   **Earth stood hard as iron,**
8   **Water like a stone.**
9
10   **Snow had fallen, snow on snow,**
11   **Snow on snow,**
12   **In the bleak midwinter**
13   **Long ago.**
14
15   **Our God, heaven cannot hold him**
16   **Nor earth sustain;**
17   **Heav'n and earth shall welcome him**
18   **When he comes to reign:**
19
20   **In the bleak midwinter**
21   **A stable place sufficed.**
22   **The Lord God incarnate,**
23   **Jesus Christ.**
24
25   **What can I give him, poor as I am?**
26   **If I were a shepherd,**
27   **I would bring a lamp;**
28   **If I were a wise man,**
29   **I would do my part;**
30   **Ye what I can, I give him:**
31   **Give my heart.**
32   *(At the close of the hymn, SECOND VOICE comes in, holding*
33   *the bundled Christ child, and gives him to MARY. The*
34   *CHILDREN'S CHOIR surrounds her, holding her arm, her*
35   *hand, her clothes. They're looking up at the baby and talking*

1   *excitedly. Each child is holding a handful of straw. They walk*
2   *toward the stable.)*
3   **SECOND VOICE:**   **Mary gave birth to her firstborn. A son.**
4   **She wrapped him in swaddling clothes.** *(JOSEPH moves*
5   *to take the child. He doesn't know how to hold a baby. There are*
6   *several false starts as he tries to take him. The CHILDREN enjoy*
7   *this. Finally he has the bundle secure. He looks at MARY and*
8   *smiles.)*
9   **JOSEPH:**   **We had to lay him in a manger.** *(He feels the pain of*
10   *this.)* **There was no room for us at the inn.** *(The pianist*
11   *plays "Away in a Manger" softly. Members of the CHILDREN'S*
12   *CHOIR, one by one, drop their handfuls of straw into the empty*
13   *manger. When they are done, they sing "Away in a Manger."*
14   *During the carol, THIRD VOICE enters with a basket of straw.*
15   *He goes to the top of the aisles and invites the children in the*
16   *congregation to take a handful of straw and place it in the*
17   *manger.)*
18   *SONG:*   "Away in a Manger."
19   **CHILDREN'S CHOIR:**   *(Singing)* **Away in a manger, no crib**
20   **for a bed,**
21   **The little Lord Jesus laid down his sweet head,**
22   **The stars in the sky looked down where he lay,**
23   **The little Lord Jesus, asleep on the hay.**
24
25   **The cattle are lowing, the baby awakes,**
26   **The little Lord Jesus, no crying he makes.**
27   **I love thee, Lord Jesus, look down from the sky,**
28   **And stay by my cradle till morning is nigh.**
29
30   **Be near me, Lord Jesus, I ask thee to stay**
31   **Close by me forever, and love me, I pray.**
32   **Bless all the dear children in thy tender care,**
33   **And fit us for heaven to live with thee there.**
34   *(When the CHILDREN'S CHOIR is through singing, they turn*
35   *and watch JOSEPH as he tenderly places the child in the manger.*

1   *The pianist plays "Thou Didst Leave Thy Throne" softly.*
2   *SECOND VOICE and THIRD VOICE place the figures of Mary,*
3   *Joseph and the Christ child in the Nativity set stable. FIRST*
4   *VOICE comes in. All watch him as he lights the Christ candle.)*
5   **FIRST VOICE:**   "My eyes have seen your salvation, which you
6   **have prepared in the presence of all people. A light for**
7   **a revelation to the Gentiles. And glory for your people**
8   **Israel."** (Luke 2:30-32)
9   *(The CHOIR or SOLOIST sings "Thou Didst Leave Thy Throne."*
10   *During the hymn, the CHILDREN'S CHOIR exits. [They can*
11   *join parents or go to a reserved pew with adult.] The VOICES*
12   *light smaller candles from the Christ candle and move out into*
13   *the aisles. The congregation can then take the small candles*
14   *placed in the pews and light them with the VOICES' candles.)*
15   *SONG:*   "Thou Didst Leave Thy Throne."
16   **CHOIR or SOLOIST:**   *(Singing)* **Thou didst leave thy throne**
17   **and thy kingly crown,**
18   **When thou camest to earth for me;**
19   **But in Bethlehem's home there was found no room**
20   **For thy holy Nativity.**
21
22   *REFRAIN:*   **O come to my heart, Lord Jesus;**
23   **There is room in my heart for thee.**
24
25   **Heaven's arches rang when the angels sang,**
26   **Proclaiming thy royal degree;**
27   **But in lowly birth didst thou come to earth,**
28   **And in great humility.**
29   *(Repeat REFRAIN.)*
30
31   **The foxes found rest, and the birds their nest**
32   **In the shade of the forest tree;**
33   **But thy couch was the sod, O thou Son of God,**
34   **In the deserts of Galilee.**
35   *(Repeat REFRAIN.)*

1	*(At the close of the hymn, the sanctuary is in candlelight only.*
2	*The CHOIR and CONGREGATION should all have their*
3	*candles lit.)*
4	**SECOND VOICE:** **"Through the tender mercy of our God, the**
5	**day has dawned upon us from on high — to give light to**
6	**those who sit in darkness and the shadow of death, and**
7	**to guide our feet in the way of peace."** (Luke 1:78-79)
8	*(CONGREGATION and CHOIR stand and sing "Silent Night"*
9	*a cappella. The VOICES exit.)*
10	*SONG:* "Silent Night."
11	**CONGREGATION/CHOIR:** *(Singing)* **Silent night! Holy night!**
12	**All is calm, all is bright**
13	**Round yon virgin mother and child,**
14	**Holy Infant, so tender and mild,**
15	**Sleep in heavenly peace,**
16	**Sleep in heavenly peace.**
17	
18	**Silent night! Holy night!**
19	**Shepherds quake at the sight!**
20	**Glories stream from heaven afar;**
21	**Heav'nly hosts sing, Alleluia!**
22	**Christ, the Savior, is born!**
23	**Christ, the Savior, is born!**
24	
25	**Silent night! Holy night!**
26	**Son of God, love's pure light**
27	**Radiant beams from thy holy face,**
28	**With the dawn of redeeming grace,**
29	**Jesus, Lord, at thy birth;**
30	**Jesus, Lord, at thy birth.**
31	*(At the close of the carol, the MINISTER stands.)*
32	**MINISTER:** **"It is not ourselves we proclaim. We proclaim**
33	**Christ Jesus as Lord, and ourselves as your servants, for**
34	**Jesus' sake. For the same God who said, 'Out of darkness**
35	**let light shine,' has caused his light to shine within us, to**

give the light of revelation — the revelation of the glory of God in the face of **Jesus Christ.**" (2 Corinthians 4:5-6)

1	**FOURTH VERSE**
2	"The Shepherds and the Angels"
3	
4	*(The lights come up, but not fully. FIRST VOICE enters.)*
5	**FIRST VOICE: "The Shepherds and the Angels."** *(FIRST*
6	*VOICE exits. A DUET stands and sings "The First Noel." The*
7	*CONGREGATION and CHOIR blow out their candles.)*
8	*SONG:* "The First Noel."
9	**DUET:** *(Singing)* **The first Noel the angels did say**
10	**Was to certain poor shepherds in fields as they lay;**
11	**In fields where they lay keeping their sheep,**
12	**On a cold winter's night that was so deep.**
13	
14	**Noel, Noel, Noel, Noel,**
15	**Born is the King of Israel.**
16	
17	**They looked up and saw a star**
18	**Bright in the east beyond them far,**
19	**And to the earth it gave great light,**
20	**And so it continued both day and night.**
21	
22	**Noel, Noel, Noel, Noel,**
23	**Born is the King of Israel.**
24	*(At the close of the carol, the SHEPHERDS enter from the back*
25	*of the sanctuary. They shout out their lines like town criers.)*
26	**SHEPHERD ONE: And there were in that same country**
27	**shepherds out in the fields . . .**
28	**SHEPHERD TWO: Keeping watch over their flocks by night!**
29	**SHEPHERD THREE: An angel of the Lord appeared to them . . .**
30	**SHEPHERD ONE: And the glory of the Lord shone all around**
31	**them . . .**
32	**SHEPHERD TWO:** *(Normal voice)* **And they were terrified.**
33	*(Suddenly a bright light hits them. It is accompanied by a loud*
34	*piano chord. The SHEPHERDS freeze in terror. Another piano*
35	*chord. They look at each other. Another chord. They look up. The*

1   *CHOIR and CONGREGATION immediately break into "Hark!*

2   *the Herald Angels Sing." The SHEPHERDS jump, startled.*

3   *They gaze at the angel voices all around them.)*

4   **SONG:**   "Hark! the Herald Angels Sing." *(First verse)*

5   **CONGREGATION/CHOIR:**   *(Singing)* **Hark! the herald angels**

6   **sing:**

7   **"Glory to the newborn King!**

8   **Peace on earth, and mercy mild;**

9   **God and sinners reconciled."**

10   **Joyful, all ye nations rise;**

11   **Join the triumph of the skies;**

12   **With th' angelic hosts proclaim,**

13   **"Christ is born in Bethlehem."**

14   **Hark! the herald angels sing,**

15   **"Glory to the newborn King."**

16   *(At the second verse, only the CHOIR WOMEN sing, pianissimo.)*

17   **CHOIR MEN:**   *(Spoken over the carol)* **Don't be afraid! Listen, I**

18   **bring you good news of great joy which will be for all**

19   **people. To you is born this day in the City of David a**

20   **Savior, who is Christ the Lord. And this will be a sign**

21   **for you: You will find the baby wrapped in swaddling**

22   **clothes and lying in a manger.**

23   **SONG:**   "Hark! the Herald Angels Sing." *(Second verse)*

24   **CHOIR WOMEN:**   *(Singing)* **Christ, by highest heav'n adored;**

25   **Christ, the everlasting Lord!**

26   **Long desired, behold him come,**

27   **Finding here his humble home.**

28   **Veiled in flesh the Godhead see;**

29   **Hail th' incarnate Deity!**

30   **Pleased as man with men to dwell,**

31   **Jesus, our Immanuel!**

32   **Hark! the herald angels sing,**

33   **"Glory to the newborn King."**

34   *(The pianist continues with bridging music.)*

35   **SHEPHERD ONE:**   **And suddenly there was with the angel a**

1   multitude of the heavenly host, praising God and saying:

2   **CHOIR:** *(Spoken or sung)* **"Glory to God in the highest! And**
3   **peace on earth among people of good will!"** *(The CHOIR*
4   *and CONGREGATION sing the final verse of "Hark! the Herald*
5   *Angels Sing.")*

6   *SONG:* "Hark! the Herald Angels Sing." *(Third verse)*

7   **CONGREGATION/CHOIR:** *(Singing)* **Hail, the heav'n-born**
8   **Prince of Peace!**
9   **Hail, the Sun of Righteousness!**
10   **Light and life to all he brings,**
11   **Ris'n with healing in his wings.**
12   **Let us then with angels sing:**
13   **"Glory to the newborn King!**
14   **Peace on earth, and mercy mild;**
15   **God and sinners reconciled."**

16   *(At the close of the carol, the bright light on the SHEPHERDS*
17   *fades. The SHEPHERDS look at each other, amazed.)*

18   **SHEPHERD ONE:** When the angels went away from them
19   into heaven, the shepherds said to one another:

20   **SHEPHERD TWO:** "Let's go over to Bethlehem and see this
21   thing that has happened, which the Lord has made
22   known to us." *(The SHEPHERDS go toward MARY and*
23   *JOSEPH.)*

24   **SHEPHERD THREE:** And they hurried off, and found Mary
25   and Joseph, and the baby... *(Smiles)* ...lying in a
26   manger. *(The pianist plays "Lullay, Lully," softly [or another*
27   *"lullaby" carol]. The SHEPHERDS kneel at the manger.*
28   *SHEPHERD ONE takes the baby into his or her arms. They*
29   *touch and kiss him. They leave gifts of milk, cheese, bread.)*

30   **JOSEPH:** And when they had seen him, they made known
31   what they had been told about the child. And all who
32   heard it wondered at what the shepherds told them.
33   *(SHEPHERD ONE gives the baby to MARY.)*

34   **MARY:** But Mary kept all these things, and they became
35   precious in her heart. *(The SHEPHERDS and JOSEPH*

1   *become a tableau. MARY or a SOLOIST sings "What Child Is*
2   *This?" [or another lullaby carol].)*
3   **SONG:** "What Child Is This?"
4   **MARY or SOLOIST:**   *(Singing)* **What Child is this, who, laid to**
5   **rest,**
6   **On Mary's lap is sleeping?**
7   **Whom angels greet with anthems sweet,**
8   **While shepherds watch are keeping?**
9   *REFRAIN:*   **This, this is Christ the King,**
10   **Whom shepherds guard and angels sing.**
11   **Haste, haste to bring him laud,**
12   **The Babe, the Son of Mary.**
13
14   **Why lies he in such mean estate**
15   **Where ox and ass are feeding?**
16   **Good Christian, fear; for sinners here**
17   **The silent Word is pleading.**
18   *(Repeat REFRAIN.)*
19
20   **So bring him incense, gold, and myrrh.**
21   **Come, peasant, King to own him.**
22   **The King of Kings salvation brings;**
23   **Let loving hearts enthrone him.**
24   *(Repeat REFRAIN.)*
25   *(At the close of the carol, there is a pause. Then the pianist begins*
26   *the bright opening to "Angels We Have Heard on High." The*
27   *SHEPHERDS rise and go to the Nativity set. They place the*
28   *shepherd and sheep figures in their proper places. They come out*
29   *into the congregation with great excitement.)*
30   **SHEPHERD ONE:**   **And the shepherds returned!**
31   **SHEPHERD TWO:**   **Glorifying and praising God for all they**
32   **had heard and seen!**
33   **SHEPHERD THREE:**   **Which happened just as it had been**
34   **told to them!** *(The CHOIR, SHEPHERDS and*
35   *CONGREGATION sing "Angels We Have Heard on High." The*

1   *SHEPHERDS move out into the aisles, stopping to sing with*
2   *members of the CONGREGATION.)*
3 *SONG:*   "Angels We Have Heard on High."
4 **CONGREGATION/SHEPHERDS/CHOIR:**   *(Singing)* **Angels we**
5   **have heard on high,**
6   **Sweetly singing o'er the plains,**
7   **And the mountains in reply,**
8   **Echoing their joyous strains.**
9 *REFRAIN:*   **Gloria in excelsis Deo!**
10   **Gloria in excelsis Deo!**
11
12   **Shepherds, why this jubilee?**
13   **Why your joyous strains prolong?**
14   **What the gladsome tidings be**
15   **Which inspire your heav'nly song?**
16   *(Repeat REFRAIN.)*
17
18   **Come to Bethlehem, and see**
19   **Him whose birth the angels sing;**
20   **Come, adore on bended knee**
21   **Christ the Lord, the newborn King.**
22   *(Repeat REFRAIN.)*
23
24
25
26
27
28
29
30
31
32
33
34
35

FIFTH VERSE

"Star of Wonder"

(At this point, the MINISTER or SPEAKER can present a short sermon or homily, if that is desired. At the close of this, the pianist begins to play "We Three Kings" softly. The VOICES enter. FIRST VOICE steps forward.)

FIRST VOICE: **"Star of Wonder."**

THIRD VOICE: **Now when Jesus was born in Bethlehem of Judea, during the reign of Herod the king, Magi came from the east to Jerusalem, saying:**

MAGUS ONE: *(From the back of the sanctuary)* **Where is the one who has been born King of the Jews?** *(The MAGI proceed up the aisle. As the MAGI speak, SECOND VOICE puts on a bright robe and becomes HEROD. FIRST VOICE and THIRD VOICE kneel on one knee. HEROD stands on their raised knees, haughtily looking down on the MAGI.)*

MAGUS TWO: **We have seen his star in the east.**

MAGUS THREE: **And have come to worship him.** *(HEROD signals angrily. The pianist abruptly stops playing.)*

HEROD: **When Herod heard this, he was disturbed, and all Jerusalem with him. And assembling all the chief priests and scribes of the people, he asked them where the Christ was to be born. They told him:**

CHOIR: **"In Bethlehem of Judea. So it was written by the prophet."**

FIRST VOICE: **"And you, Bethlehem, in the land of Judah, are by no means the least among the rulers of Judah.**

THIRD VOICE: **"For from you shall come a ruler who will govern my people Israel."** (Micah 5:2)

HEROD: **Then Herod summoned the Magi secretly and ascertained from them the exact time the star had appeared. He then sent them to Bethlehem.** *(Maliciously)* **"Go and search thoroughly for the child! And when you have found him, bring the news back to me, so I, too, may**

223

1   **go and . . . worship him."** *(The pianist begins playing "We*
2   *Three Kings," louder this time.)*
3   **SECOND VOICE:** *(Taking off the robe)* **When they had heard**
4   **the king, they went their way.** *(A MEN'S TRIO sings the*
5   *first verse of "We Three Kings." During this, the MAGI process*
6   *down an aisle. They are discussing something among themselves.*
7   *One unrolls and holds a star chart for the others to see. One of*
8   *them points up. They see the star. They turn and follow the star,*
9   *eyes always up to heaven.)*
10   *SONG:*   "We Three Kings."
11   **MEN'S TRIO:**   *(Singing)* **We three kings of Orient are;**
12   **Bearing gifts we traverse afar,**
13   **Field and fountain, moor and mountain,**
14   **Following yonder star.**
15   *REFRAIN:*   **O star of wonder, star of night,**
16   **Star with royal beauty bright,**
17   **Westward leading, still proceeding,**
18   **Guide us to thy perfect light.**
19   *(At the close of the first verse and refrain, the MEN'S TRIO stops*
20   *singing while the pianist continues to play softly.)*
21   **FIRST VOICE:**   **Look! The star they had first seen in the east**
22   **now went before them, until it stood above the place**
23   **where the child rested.** *(The MAGI stop and look down from*
24   *the sky. They are looking at MARY, JOSEPH and the Christ*
25   *child. MARY and JOSEPH are looking back at them curiously.*
26   *The MAGI draw near to them.)*
27   **SECOND VOICE:**   **When they saw the star, they rejoiced with**
28   **great joy and went into the house. There they saw the**
29   **child with his mother, and they fell down and worshiped**
30   **him.** *(The MAGI kneel down, then lean forward and touch their*
31   *foreheads to the ground, hands outstretched in front. Then they*
32   *sit up and lay their gifts in front of the mother and child.)*
33   **THIRD VOICE:**   **Then, opening up their strongboxes, they**
34   **offered him gifts. Gold. Frankincense. And myrrh.** *(The*
35   *MAGI bow and stand.)* **And having been warned in a dream**

1   **not to return to Herod, they departed to their own**
2   **country by another road.** *(The MAGI go to the Nativity set*
3   *and place figures of themselves in the scene. The MAGI leave*
4   *down a side aisle. The MEN'S TRIO continues "We Three Kings,"*
5   *with the CHOIR joining on the refrain. During the carol, MARY*
6   *and JOSEPH and the VOICES exit.*
7   *(The offering can be taken at this time. Ushers may either pass*
8   *the offering plates, or better still, set the collection plates at the*
9   *front of the church and let the CONGREGATION come forward*
10 *to offer their gifts. Christmas presents for the clergy and staff*
11 *may also be offered at this time.)*
12 *SONG:* "We Three Kings." *(Verses two-five)*
13 **MEN'S TRIO:** *(Singing)* **Born a King on Bethlehem's plain,**
14 **Gold I bring to crown him again,**
15 **King forever, ceasing never,**
16 **Over us all to reign.**
17 *(TRIO and CHOIR sing REFRAIN.)*
18
19 *(MEN'S TRIO)* **Frankincense to offer have I;**
20 **Incense owns a Deity nigh;**
21 **Prayer and praising gladly raising,**
22 **Worship him, God most high.**
23 *(TRIO and CHOIR sing REFRAIN.)*
24
25 *(MEN'S TRIO)* **Myrrh is mine: its bitter perfume**
26 **Breathes a life of gathering gloom:**
27 **Sorrowing, sighing, bleeding, dying,**
28 **Sealed in the stone-cold tomb.**
29 *(TRIO and CHOIR sing REFRAIN.)*
30
31 *(MEN'S TRIO)* **Glorious now behold him arise,**
32 **King and God and sacrifice;**
33 **Alleluia, Alleluia!**
34 **Sounds through the earth and skies.**
35 *(TRIO and CHOIR sing REFRAIN.)*

1   *(The CHOIR can continue with "Brightest and Best.")*

2   ***SONG:***   "Brightest and Best."

3   **CHOIR:**   *(Singing)* **Brightest and best are the stars of the morning,**

4   **Dawn on our darkness, and lend us thine aid;**

5   **Star of the east, the horizon adorning,**

6   **Guide where our infant Redeemer is laid.**

7

8   **Cold on the cradle and dewdrops are shining;**

9   **Low lies his head with the beasts of the stall;**

10   **Angels adore him in slumber reclining,**

11   **Maker and Monarch and Savior of all.**

12

13   **Shall we then yield him, in costly devotion,**

14   **Odors of Edom, and offerings divine,**

15   **Gems of the mountain and pearls of the ocean,**

16   **Myrrh from the forest and gold from the mine?**

17

18   **Vainly we offer each ample oblation;**

19   **Vainly with gifts would his favor secure;**

20   **Richer by far is the heart's adoration,**

21   **Dearer to God are the prayers of the poor.**

22   *(Optional: This may be followed by a SOLOIST singing "I*

23   *Wonder As I Wander." At the close of the carol, FIRST VOICE*

24   *enters and comes forward.)*

25   **FIRST VOICE:**   "The shepherds sing; and shall I silent be?

26   My God, no hymn for thee? My soul's a shepherd too; a

27   flock it feeds of thoughts, and words, and deeds. The

28   pasture is thy word: the streams, thy grace — enriching

29   all the place!"* *(The pianist begins the first bright chords of*

30   *"Joy to the World.")*

31   ***SONG:***   "Joy to the World."

32   **CONGREGATION/CHOIR:**   *(Singing)* **Joy to the world! the**

33

34   **"Christmas" by George Herbert. George Herbert and the 17th-Century Religious*

       Poets, edited by Mario A. DiCesare and published by W. W. Norton & Company,

35   *Inc., New York, 1978.*

1   Lord is come:
2   Let earth receive her King;
3   Let ev'ry heart prepare him room,
4   And heaven and nature sing,
5   And heaven and nature sing,
6   And heaven, and heaven and nature sing.
7
8   Joy to the world! the Savior reigns:
9   Let men their songs employ;
10   While fields and floods, rocks, hills, and plains
11   Repeat the sounding joy,
12   Repeat the sounding joy,
13   Repeat, repeat the sounding joy.
14
15   No more let sin and sorrow grow,
16   Nor thorns infest the ground;
17   He comes to make his blessings flow
18   Far as the curse is found,
19   Far as the curse is found,
20   Far as, far as the curse is found.
21
22   He rules the world with truth and grace,
23   And makes the nations prove
24   The glories of his righteousness,
25   And wonders of his love,
26   And wonders of his love,
27   And wonders, wonders of his love.
28   *(As the CONGREGATION and CHOIR sing, they should be*
29   *encouraged to greet each other, offering gifts they've brought for*
30   *one another. If desired, the CONGREGATION can be encouraged*
31   *to move around the sanctuary. This is, after all, a celebration.*
32   *Carols, hymns and worship songs of similar brightness may*
33   *follow.)*
34
35

1	**TO CODA**
2	**"Come, Thou Long-Expected Jesus"**
3	
4	*(After the CONGREGATION has settled, the pianist begins*
5	*playing "Come, Thou Long-Expected Jesus." The VOICES enter*
6	*and move to the front, as in the beginning.)*
7	**FIRST VOICE: Christmas is nearly here:**
8	**A time of celebration**
9	**For the star, the angels,**
10	**The manger.**
11	**But another memory greets this**
12	**Season.**
13	**One we sometimes forget.**
14	**The Baby in Bethlehem was born**
15	**For one reason.**
16	**To die.**
17	**SECOND VOICE: Once we were a people huddled in**
18	**Darkness.**
19	**Now we are those who glory in**
20	**The light.**
21	**THIRD VOICE: Once we were a people who prayed**
22	**For salvation.**
23	**Now we are those who worship with**
24	**Clean hearts.**
25	**FIRST VOICE: Once we were a people who looked**
26	**For a Savior.**
27	**Now we are those who wait for his**
28	**Return.**
29	*(The CONGREGATION and CHOIR sing "Come, Thou Long-*
30	*Expected Jesus.")*
31	*SONG:* "Come, Thou Long-Expected Jesus."
32	**CONGREGATION/CHOIR:** *(Singing)* **Come, thou long-expected**
33	**Jesus,**
34	**Born to set thy people free;**
35	**From our fears and sins release us;**

228

1   **Let us find our rest in thee.**
2   **Israel's strength and consolation,**
3   **Hope of all the earth thou art;**
4   **Dear desire of every nation,**
5   **Joy of every longing heart.**
6
7   **Born thy people to deliver,**
8   **Born a child and yet a King,**
9   **Born to reign in us forever,**
10   **Now thy gracious kingdom bring.**
11   **By thine own eternal spirit**
12   **Rule in all our hearts alone;**
13   **By thine all sufficient merit,**
14   **Raise us to thy glorious throne.**
15   *(At the close of the hymn, the MINISTER may offer a benediction.*
16   *The final carol may be "O Come, All Ye Faithful" or another*
17   *song of worshipful celebration. Bright music is played as the*
18   *congregation leaves.)*
19
20
21
22
23
24
25
26
27
28
29
30
31
32
33
34
35

ABOUT THE AUTHORS

Photo: Drew Meredith

Larry and Annie Enscoe are the authors of eleven books of Christian drama — including a best-selling Christmas (*Wrappings*) and Easter (*First Light*) collection that is performed all over the world.

You Can Get There From Here, their book of teen issue plays, garnered an Angel Award. *Thunder at Dawn,* a full-length Easter play, continues to be performed in theatres throughout the United States and Canada.

They have also written scripts for Josh McDowell and the Dove Award-winning filmmaker, Ken Carpenter.

Larry and Annie have been writing and producing Christmas programs for Glendale Presbyterian Church since 1989.

The Enscoes make their home in Pasadena where they write for film and television, as well as the live stage. Larry studied dramatic arts at Westmont College and the University of California at Berkeley. He is a former member of the Los Angeles Drama Critics Circle and was a theatre critic for the Los Angeles Daily News. Annie studied education and theatre at Wheaton College. She has taught drama in both the classroom and seminar settings.

CASTS
OF
ORIGINAL
PRODUCTIONS

Call for the Lights and Sing! was first performed on December 10, 1989 at Glendale Presbyterian Church in Glendale, California, with the following cast:

KNAVE ONE	Larry Enscoe
KNAVE TWO	Eric Loomis
KNAVE THREE	Jeff Witzeman
KING	Dan McGowan
QUEEN	Noel Schnedl
CHOIR MISTRESS	Nancee Olsen
THE PARSON	Rev. Jack Chisholm
THE JUGGLER	Greg Godwin
MUSICIANS OF THE HALL	Corey Gemme, Alan Parr, Ron Christian, Harold Garrett, John West

THE CATHEDRAL CHOIR (Nancee Olsen — Director)
THE SOJOURNER SINGERS (Nancee Olsen — Director)

Call for the Lights and Sing! was written and directed by Larry & Annie Enscoe. Produced by Nancee Olsen. Musical direction by Nancee Olsen. Set design by Lynn Flett. Lighting and sound design by Jim Collins.

The Wise Men Had It Easy was first performed on December 9, 1990 at Glendale Presbyterian Church in Glendale, California, with the following cast:

THE DIRECTOR	Larry Enscoe
SHOPPER ONE	Lori Thomley
SHOPPER TWO	Rick Olson
SHOPPER THREE	Eric Loomis
SALESMAN	Eric Loomis
FUNNY GUY ONE	Drew Meredith
FUNNY GUY TWO	Eric Loomis
KID WITH A BALLOON	David Watrous
KID ONE	Katie Prosser
KID TWO	Katie Engel

THE CATHEDRAL CHOIR (Claire Collins — Director)
THE SOJOURNER SINGERS (Jannette Bishop — Director)
THE CHORISTER CHOIR (Jannette Bishop — Director)
THE CAROL CHOIR (Joann Hannaford — Director)

The Wise Men Had It Easy was written and directed by Larry & Annie Enscoe. Music selection and direction by Claire Collins. Musical accompaniment by John West. Lighting and sound design by Jim Collins.

The King Who Hated Christmas was first performed on December 15, 1991 at Glendale Presbyterian Church in Glendale, California, with the following cast:

SAMMY	Andrew Tibert
DAVIS	David Cassell
GWEN	Lauren Down
KING CORNELIUS	Larry Enscoe
LUMP	Drew Meredith
SERVANT ONE	Chris Clark
SERVANT TWO	Bruce Dunham
MUSIC MEISTER	Kevin Hofer
VILLAGE CHILDREN	Kelly Scheetz, Jimmy VanDeventer, David Watrous
VILLAGE ONE	Beth Winter
VILLAGE CHILD TWO	Rachel Down
LITTLE GIRL	Lisa Rowland
MRS. O'CEDAR	Cathye Curreri
VILLAGE MATRIARCH	Marilyn Austin
ORCHESTRA	John West, Steve Williams, Alice Rucker, Dane Nelsen, Mike Andreas, Stuart Appekar, John McIntyre

THE CATHEDRAL CHOIR (Kevin Hofer — Director)
THE YOUNG PEOPLE'S MUSIC MACHINE — (John West — Director)
THE KINGDOM KIDS — Dan McGowan — Director)

The King Who Hated Christmas was written and directed by Larry & Annie Enscoe. Musical direction by Kevin Hofer. Lighting design by Nancy Blumstein and Jim Collins. Sound design by Jim Collins. Set design by Chris Clark, Gary Hopkins, Nancy Tibert, Laurianne Williams, Lynn Flett.

The Great Gemdale Christmas Tree Ornament Factory
was first performed on December 11, 1993 at Glendale Presbyterian Church in Glendale, California, with the following cast:

GRAMMIE	Gerry Rogers
LISA	Natalie Raasch
JENNY	Lonna Pritchard
MS. PEEVISH	Dana Beth Benningfield
SHRILL	Jose Rivera
CHRISTMAS STRANGER	Steve Craig
FACTORY FIVE PLUS ONE ORCHESTRA	Kemp Smeal, Steve Williams, John Graff, Tish Racheli, John Nelson, Kevin Hofer

THE CATHEDRAL CHOIR (Kevin Hofer — Director)

CROSS WALK (Dan McGowan — Director)

YOUNG RHEE

HOGAR CRISTIANO CHOIR (Rodrigo Flores — Director)

MAHER & FADI BATERSEH

HYAVED ARMENIAN CHURCH CHOIR (Sam Agulian — Director)

FIRST EVANGELICAL FREE CHINESE CHURCH CHILDRENS CHOIR (Lilly Lou — Director)

The Great Gemdale Christmas Tree Ornament Factory
was written by Larry & Annie Enscoe. Directed by Barry Pintar.
Musical direction by Kevin Hofer. Produced by Kevin Hofer. Set
design by Dan McGowan. Lighting design by Don Wolford.

The Towne Without a Tale was first performed on December 10, 1993 at Glendale Presbyterian Church in Glendale, California, with the following cast:

NIGHT WATCHMAN	Drew Meredith
DUNLEY	Dean Batali
STREET URCHIN	David Watrous
VILLAGE MAYOR	Darrell Johnson
OLD MAN WINTER	Ralph Winter
OLIVE	Laura Hill
MIKE	Larry Enscoe
DENNIS	Cameron Carothers
BRIAN	Kevin King
THE ORCHESTRA	Kemp Smeal, Steve Williams, John Nelson, Frank Dutro
THE EARLY MUSIC ENSEMBLE	Sally Cadwell, Ned Boyer, Eva Marghazi

THE CATHEDRAL CHOIR (Bob Hogins — Director)
THE MADRIGAL SINGERS (Bob Hogins — Director)

The Towne Without a Tale was written and directed by Larry & Annie Enscoe. Produced by Laurianne Williams. Musical direction by Bob Hogins. Lighting design by Drew and Brenna Meredith. Sound design by Carl Lange. Set design by LindaAnn Napolitano, Bill Serafini, Gary Hopkins, Victoria Winter.

ORDER FORM

MERIWETHER PUBLISHING LTD.
P.O. BOX 7710
COLORADO SPRINGS, CO 80933
TELEPHONE: (719) 594-4422

Please send me the following books:

_____**Joy to the World! #CC-B161**   **$12.95**
by L. G. Enscoe and Annie Enscoe
A variety collection of Christmas programs

_____**Christmas on Stage #CC-B153**   **$14.95**
by Theodore O. Zapel
An anthology of Christmas plays for performance

_____**Get a Grip! #CC-B128**   **$9.95**
by L. G. Enscoe and Annie Enscoe
Contemporary scenes and monologs for Christian teens

_____**Divine Comedies #CC-B190**   **$12.95**
by T. M. Williams
A collection of plays for church drama groups

_____**Teaching With Bible Games #CC-B108**   **$10.95**
by Ed Dunlop
20 "kid-tested" contests for Christian education

_____**Storytelling From the Bible #CC-B145**   **$10.95**
by Janet Litherland
The art of biblical storytelling

_____**Costuming the Christmas and Easter Play**   **$7.95**
by Alice M. Staeheli #CC-B180
How to costume any religious play

**These and other fine Meriwether Publishing books are available at
your local Christian bookstore or direct from the publisher. Use the
handy order form on this page.**

NAME: _____

ORGANIZATION NAME: _____

ADDRESS: _____

CITY: _____ STATE: _____ ZIP: _____

PHONE: _____

☐ **Check Enclosed**
☐ **Visa or MasterCard #**_____

*Signature:*_____ *Expiration
Date:*_____

(required for Visa/MasterCard orders)

COLORADO RESIDENTS: Please add 3% sales tax.
SHIPPING: Include $2.75 for the first book and 50¢ for each additional book ordered.

☐ *Please send me a copy of your complete catalog of books and plays.*